LAN

DISASTER
PREVENTION
AND RECOVERY

PATRICK H. CORRIGAN

PTR Prentice Hall
Englewood Cliffs, NJ 07632

Library of Congress Cataloging-in-Publication Data

Corrigan, Patrick H.
LAN disaster prevention and recovery / Patrick H. Corrigan.
    p.   cm.
Includes index.
ISBN 0-13-015819-4
    1. Local area networks (Computer Networks)--Maintenance and repair.   2. Local area networks (Computer networks)--Security measures.   I. Title.
TK5105.7.C685   1994
658.4'78--dc20

94-868
CIP

Editorial/Production Supervision: Lisa Iarkowski
Interior "Connected Computers" design: Gail Cocker-Bogusz
Acquisitions Editor: Mary Franz
Manufacturing Manager: Alexis R. Heydt
Cover Photo: The Image Bank, James Noel Smith
Cover Design: Design Solutions

The publisher offers discounts on this book when ordered in bulk quantities. For more information, contact:

Corporate Sales Department
PTR Prentice Hall
113 Sylvan Avenue
Englewood Cliffs, NJ 07632
Phone: 201-592-2863
FAX: 201-592-2249.

Printed in the United States of America

10 9 8 7 6 5 4 3 2 1

ISBN 0-13-015819-4

Prentice-Hall International (UK) Limited, London
Prentice-Hall of Australia Pty. Limited, Sydney
Prentice-Hall of Canada, Inc., Toronto
Prentice-Hall Hispanoamericana S.A., Mexico
Prentice-Hall of India Private Limited, New Delhi
Prentice-Hall of Japan, Inc., Tokyo
Simon & Schuster Asia Pte. Ltd., Singapore
Editora Prentice-Hall do Brasil, Ltda., Rio de Janeiro

Trademarks

123 is a trademark of Lotus Development Corporation
ARCserve is a trademark of Cheyenne Software
ADSTAR Distributed Storage Manager is a trademark of IBM
Bindview NCS is a trademark of LAN Support Group
Btrieve is a trademark of Novell, Inc.
Cheyenne Utilities is a trademark of Cheyenne Software
Close-Up is a trademark of Norton-Lambert Corporation
DBagent is a trademark of Cheyenne Software
Digital Linear Tape is a trademark of Digital Equipment Corporation
ESM is a trademark of Legent Corporation
Flex/QL is a trademark of DataAccess Corporation
Folio Views is a trademark of Folio Corporation
FOR/UPSTREAM is a trademark of Innovation Data Processing
LAN Auditor is a trademark of Horizons Technology, Inc.
LAN Automatic Inventory is a trademark of Brightwork Development Corporation
LAN^{2}LAN is a trademark of Newport Systems Solutions
Legato Networker is a trademark of Legato Systems, Inc.
Magic is a trademark of Magic Software Enterprises, Inc.
MasterDAT is a trademark of GigaTrend, Inc.
Microsoft Windows is a trademark of Microsoft Corporation
MPR is a trademark of Novell, Inc.
MT-350 is a trademark of Microtest, Inc.
NetWare is a trademark of Novell, Inc.
Network Archivist is a trademark of Palindrome, Inc.
Network HQ is a trademark of MAGEE Enterprises
ORACLE Server is a trademark of Oracle Corporation
OS/2 is a trademark of IBM Corporation
PC Anywhere is a trademark of Symantec, Inc.
PC Census is a trademark of Talley Systems Corporation
PKZIP is a trademark of PKWARE, Inc.
PNA is a trademark of Palindrome Corporation
P-Touch is a trademark of Brother International Corporation
Remote LAN Node is a trademark of DCA, Inc.
R&R Report Writer is a Trademark of Concentric Data Systems, Inc.
StorageExpress is a trademark of Intel Corporation
Storage Management Services is a trademark of Novell, Inc.
TCNS is a trademark of Thomas-Conrad Corporation
TIMERUN is a trademark of Central Point Software
Unitag is a trademark of A 'n D Cable Products, Inc.
UNIX is a registered trademark of UNIX System Laboratories, Inc. (a wholly-owned subsidiary
    of Novell, Inc.)
USER-Access is a trademark of Network Systems Corporation
VINES is a trademark of Banyan Systems
VISIO is a trademark of Shapeware Corporation
WordPerfect is a trademark of WordPerfect Corporation

For my wife Karen and my son Patrick, Jr.

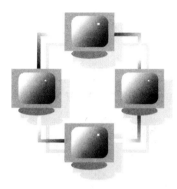

Table of Contents

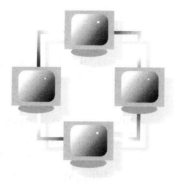

Preface

*T*o use an old cliché, LAN disaster prevention and recovery is like the weather: a lot of people talk about it, but (almost) nobody does anything about it. In some ways, this is an apt analogy, because both the weather and LANs can be affected by minute events, the results of which can be difficult to predict or control.

The vast majority of companies that use LANs have no written disaster plans, and almost all of those that do have plans only cover specific aspects of disaster prevention and recovery, such as backup and restore or off-site recovery. One of the reasons that little has been done in this area is that most people start out trying to apply the disaster planning approaches used in mainframe data centers to LANs. Unfortunately, this model only works with relatively static systems, where changes are tightly controlled from the top. Most LANs, however, are dynamic and changing, with little top-down control. A top-down, tightly controlled approach to disaster planning is either doomed to failure in a LAN environment or will kill the flexibility that LAN-based systems provide. Effective LAN disaster planning and recovery requires a new approach that allows for flexibility while still providing necessary protection against disaster. The goal of this book is to help in the development of that new approach.

This book starts with an introduction to the concepts of LAN disaster prevention and recovery and an overview of the kinds of disasters that need to be protected against. It follows with guidelines to the planning process, addressing the differences between data center disaster planning and LAN disaster planning as well as the issues of who needs to be involved and what you need to plan for. Documentation, key to not only effective disaster planning, but effective management as well, is discussed, as well as guidelines for building system reliability, the first step in disaster prevention. Another key factor in disaster prevention, security, is addressed also, followed by a discussion of data backup and recovery.

Power-related problems are something everyone knows exist, but very little information is available on their causes and cures. The discussion of power-related problems in this book will hopefully clear up some of the confusion. Unfortunately, this is not a topic where clear-cut answers are easily available.

The topic of business resumption planning is addressed next. This one subject has probably been the most difficult to address in LAN disaster plans. Finally, the focus turns to the process and mechanics of writing disaster recovery plans and includes discussions of planning tools, flow-charting and testing.

A Note About The Examples Used In This Book:

Many of the examples used in this book are based on Novell's NetWare, one of the most popular network operating systems in use today. The concepts, however, apply to most LAN environments. I hope no one feels slighted.

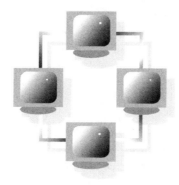

Acknowledgements

*B*ecause I have received help from so many sources, there is really no way to thank everyone who, in one manner or another, contributed to this book. There are a few people, however, who need to be singled out.

First, I would like to thank Karen, my wife and business partner. Without her efforts this book would probably have never been finished.

I would also like to thank Richard Retin and Teresa Joyce for their help. Also, without the help of Tom Shaughnessy of PowerCET Corporation and Mark Waller of The Waller Group, Chapter 7, *Power Backup and Conditioning* could not have been completed.

I especially want to thank my editor at Prentice Hall, Mary Franz, for her help and incredible patience. I would also like to thank Noreen Regina, Lisa Iarkowski and everyone else at Prentice Hall who helped with this project.

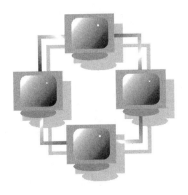

About the Author

*P*atrick H. Corrigan is the Managing Director of *The Corrigan Group*, a consulting firm based in Tigard, Oregon. He is a recognized authority on Local Area Networks, and is the author of several books and numerous articles on the topic. Mr. Corrigan lectures and teaches extensively in the areas of LAN management, planning and design as well as LAN disaster prevention and recovery. His writing has appeared in *ComputerWorld, Inc. Magazine, LAN Technology, LAN Times, Network World* and *Stacks*. His consulting work focuses on LAN system planning, design and management, LAN disaster prevention and recovery, and LAN product marketing. Mr. Corrigan can be reached via CompuServe at 75170,146.

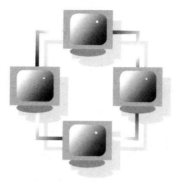

Introduction

A few short years ago, most LANs were simple systems connecting a few PCs, primarily for printer sharing and file transfer. Today, however, companies large and small rely on LAN-based systems for many or all of their data processing needs. The continued operation of the LAN is intertwined with the continued operation of the organization.

Many people think that LAN disaster prevention and recovery means performing proper backups and recovering from file server disk crashes. While these things are important, they are only part of the picture and only help with specific types of potential disasters.

LAN disaster prevention and recovery must deal with all contingencies. You must develop plans to avoid disasters as well as recover from them when (not if) they occur.

It Can't Happen Here, Can It?

It is very easy to ignore potential disasters until they happen to you. Disasters come in all shapes and sizes. They can affect one person or many. They can affect an organization's operation for a short time or force it to close its doors forever.[1] Hardware or software failure, human error and sabotage can destroy data or systems. Natural disasters and environmental contamination can make your entire business site unavailable. The question is not if disaster will strike, but when and how. Following are examples of actual

---

[1]Numerous articles and presentations have quoted statistics similar to the following:

> *43% of all businesses that suffer a major data disaster and have no tested disaster recovery plan will never reopen.*

> *90% of those companies which have no disaster recovery plan that reopen after a data disaster, will go out of business or be acquired within two years.*

Apparently, these statistics turn out to be more like the children's game of "telephone" than anything else. One researcher traced these figures back through numerous versions to a 1949 story in *The Journal of Commerce* magazine that read in part:

> *43% of companies that had a major fire and did not have adequate business interruption insurance went out of business in three years.*

Obviously, given the date, this study had nothing to do with computers and electronic data loss! (Source: Article by Ed Devlin in the Fourth Quarter, 1993 issue of *Disaster Recovery Journal*. This article is reprinted in *Appendix C*.)

The only study that the author could locate was a 1987 *survey* of mainframe data centers conducted by researchers at the University of Texas at Arlington (*Financial and Functional Impacts of Computer Outages on Business*, Steven R. Christensen, Lawrence L. Schkade and Asbel Smith). This survey asked IS managers to *estimate* the cost and impact of disaster, and gave no conclusions concerning the ability of a business to survive a data disaster.

events. In most cases, names have been omitted to protect the innocent (or guilty!).

Disaster Example #1

On Tuesday, October 17, 1989, at 5:04 p.m., a major earthquake shook Northern California. After I left my office in a high-rise building in San Francisco's Financial District, I stood looking at the bricks from the building's facade that littered the street. I then realized that all of my backup tapes were sitting on a desk next to the tape drive. Hardware, software and office furniture could be replaced, but for my consulting and training business to survive I needed my client database! At that moment I did not know how badly the building was damaged or if I would ever be able to retrieve anything from my office. I was fortunate, however. Building damage was minor, and I was able to enter and use my office on Thursday.

Disaster Example #2

During the same earthquake, an office of a San Francisco bank had their file servers on the type of open shelving units commonly called *bread racks*. One rack was on casters; the other was not. Neither rack was strapped to the wall. The server on the wheeled rack survived. The non-wheeled rack, however, tipped over, sending the server crashing to the floor, destroying its hard disks.

Disaster Example #3

At a California research firm, a service technician working on a network file server accidentally crashed both of its duplexed 600 MB (megabyte) disk drives. When the staff attempted to restore the data from tape backup, at least 150 MB of files on tape were corrupted. Although they had implemented proper backup procedures, they had never properly tested their backup system. Fortunately, in this case most of the lost data was from previously completed projects and was no longer needed. Also, the crash happened on a Friday afternoon, and they were up and running by Monday morning.

Disaster Example #4

A software development group in a large company had a file server with about 5 GB (gigabytes) of data. For some reason this server was on a dolly so that it could be rolled around the computer room. One day it was being moved while it was still running and fell off the dolly, crashing the drives. After replacing the drives, the staff attempted to restore data from tape backup. Unfortunately, the backup tape only contained the directory structure of the server, since the backup system operator did not have sufficient rights to back up any data! One year of work on a software project was lost. Because of this, the project was later canceled.

Disaster Example #5

A transformer in the basement of a university building exploded, contaminating the building with PCBs. The heating/air conditioning system carried the contamination to four other buildings, making all five uninhabitable. To this day nothing can be removed from the buildings, including computers, disks or tapes.

Disaster Example #6

A single defective Token Ring card brought down a 200+ user network. It took several hours to locate and repair the problem.

Disaster Example #7

A disgruntled system supervisor left a company and changed all supervisor-level passwords on his way out the door. Outside assistance was required to regain access. There have been numerous similar cases. Depending on the system and circumstances, the time to gain access could range from a few hours to several days.

© Joe Troise and Phil Frank

Disaster Example #8

An engineer lost several months of work when his PC hard disk crashed. Although he was connected to a network file server, he stored all of his files locally and never backed up.

Disaster Example #9

In 1992 Hurricane Andrew leveled much of Southern Florida. Many buildings were completely obliterated or severely damaged. In many cases, even if a business' facility survived, much of the staff were more worried about housing, food or other necessities than they were about business recovery. In addition, a lack of infrastructure, such as power, communications and roads, made conducting business nearly impossible.

The nearly-new office of Data Access Corporation, a software company in the South Miami area, was almost completely destroyed by the hurricane. In addition, nearly one-third of the staff, including the owners, lost their homes. Fortunately, the company regularly shipped backups of all their data, including source code, to their subsidiary in Sweden as well as a local site. They were able to get the entire staff to pitch in and gather whatever was salvageable and move to a temporary location north of Miami. They were at least partially operational within a week and were able to recover all of their data from backup tapes. Although they also kept paper backup of their accounting files, those are now "covering the Everglades." The hurricane literally blew the paper into the Everglades west of Miami.

Disaster Example #10

In June 1991, lightning struck the roof of Micro Information Systems, a LAN systems integrator in Mequon, Wisconsin. The lightning jumped to a telephone extension cable, traveled to and destroyed the telephone switch, and then traveled down a phone line to a modem in a network-attached PC. The power surge traveled on to the Thin Ethernet cable and destroyed numerous LAN cards, in one case actually blowing chips off a LAN card. In all, there was approximately $80,000 in damage. A technician who had his hand on a PC keyboard was knocked to the floor but fortunately was unhurt. (His co-workers, however, now call him "Sparky.")

Disaster Planning Objectives

A failing of traditional information systems (IS) executives in many organizations is that they consider the IS department (often called *Management Information Systems*, or *MIS*) to be separate from the rest of the company. Even the term *glass house*, commonly used to describe the IS department, promotes this view.

While doing research for this project, I made some inquiries on several CompuServe forums[2] about experiences people have had with disasters. On one forum someone mentioned the effect of Hurricane Andrew on people and businesses not directly affected by the storm. Another person responded that those effects were outside the bounds of discussion:

> *I did not mean to say that those not hit by sustained hurricane-force winds did not suffer from the storm. However, Patrick's original question was about Disaster Recovery. I capitalize this because it is a defined subject in MIS. It does **not** refer to having problems with your business or employees, but to catastrophic failure of a computer system.*

---

[2]CompuServe is an on-line information service discussed later in this book. A forum is an interest area where CompuServe users can exchange information.

The traditional MIS view is that business or personnel problems are not their concern. Computer systems are used to serve the needs of people and business, and people are needed to operate and use computers. If a business is destroyed or people are not available to get their jobs done, the computer systems are no longer important. It is important to understand how data disaster recovery fits in the overall picture of business disaster recovery.

Unlike traditional IS, the LAN has become an integral part of the company. It is the data highway that allows information to flow throughout the organization. It connects the desktop to file servers, hosts and other data resources. It is not a separate data service—it is woven throughout the fabric of the organization. As such, business disaster prevention and recovery and LAN disaster prevention and recovery are inextricably intertwined. Once you understand this, the following objective should be evident.

The Primary Objective

The primary objective of LAN disaster prevention and recovery planning is to enable a business or other organization to operate without interruption, or to resume operation after a disaster in a timely fashion.

Obviously, you are not going to solve all of your organization's problems with LAN disaster planning. By broadening the context of disaster prevention and recovery, however, you can make sure that your plans are consistent with the needs of the organization as a whole.

In order to implement effective disaster plans, you must have the cooperation and support of the entire organization, especially top management. Without management support you will not be able to accomplish your objectives. This means more than lip service; it means a willingness to commit the necessary resources, financial and other, to the project. You will also need the support of the user community, because you will need their help to build, test and implement the plans. To gain this cooperation, you will need to develop the confidence and trust of those people whose cooperation you need.

A State of Mind

Disaster prevention and recovery is not just something you do, it is a state of mind. It is a way of looking at things and dealing with situations. When you look at a system or procedure, you need to consider what can go wrong and what will happen if something goes wrong. How can you prevent problems? How can you recover from them? Who do you call for help, and will they be available in an emergency? Is there a better alternative? With practice, this approach becomes second nature and helps you prevent problems before they happen.

Disaster Planning Issues

If your plans are to be effective, they must address three major issues:

- Maintaining system availability (keeping the system functioning)
- Maintaining data integrity, availability and security
- Recovering from disaster in a timely fashion

Maintaining System Availability

Maintaining system availability first requires proper LAN planning, design and installation. A properly designed and installed physical network, including cabling, hubs, file servers, bridges and routers, will prevent many problems or make them easier to locate and troubleshoot when they occur. For the same reasons, logical structures, such as security, login scripts and directory structures, also need to be designed properly. Issues relating to system availability are discussed in Chapters 3, 4, 7 and 8.

"OH YEAH, AND TRY NOT TO ENTER THE WRONG PASSWORD."

Maintaining Data Integrity

Maintaining data integrity, like maintaining system availability, also requires proper LAN planning, design and installation. Without system integrity it is impossible to maintain data integrity. Building an effective logical structure with proper security and access control is a first step toward maintaining data integrity. Security does not just prevent unauthorized access—it can also prevent or limit accidental file deletions and the spreading of viruses. Power problems can wreak havoc with your data. Unfortunately, preventing power problems is not as simple as throwing a surge protector on each PC. As LANs grow in size and capacity, the issues of data backup become more complex. Data integrity issues are discussed in Chapters 4, 5, 6 and 7.

Recovering from Disaster in a Timely Fashion

No matter what steps you take to prevent disasters, they will happen, so you need to be prepared to recover from them in a timely fashion. Effective, well-documented data backup systems and procedures are essential. Spare equipment, such as hubs, patch cables and LAN cards, a maintenance and repair plan and a trained support staff can all play a big role in recovery. Good documentation is a must, and, for most organizations, so is an off-site business recovery plan. Recovery issues are discussed in Chapters 2, 3, 6 and 9.

Selling Disaster Prevention and Recovery

For those of you who have never wanted to be in sales, I have bad news: To build effective disaster plans you need to become salespeople. Worse yet, you need to become *insurance* salespeople! A big part of your job will be to convince people who don't like to think about disaster that it can happen to them. You also need to convince those people of the need to commit resources (including money) to the prevention of and recovery from disasters. Isn't this exactly what insurance salespeople do? More about this in Chapter 2.

What Is Downtime?

Downtime means different things to different people. To a LAN administrator, downtime often means the unavailability of a file server or major LAN component. To a user, however, downtime can mean unavailability of a specific application or peripheral, or that user's desktop computer.

For our purposes, we will use the following definition:

Downtime

Downtime is the unavailability of a computer system or portion of a computer system, including its software and peripherals, which results in a loss of productivity.

If a user cannot attach to a required printer, that's downtime. If the power goes out in the wiring closet and shuts down all the hubs, that's also downtime. If your office is in Los Angeles and California falls into the ocean, that too is downtime, although at that point you might have more important things to worry about!

What Does Downtime Cost and Why Should I Care?

You need cost figures to justify expenditures for prevention of downtime. The cost of downtime can be measured in several ways:

- Lost income
- Lost productivity
- Legal liability incurred by not meeting deadlines
- Lost clients or client confidence due to the inability to respond to their needs
- Lost user confidence due to continual downtime
- Lower corporate profitability
- Inability to compete due to higher costs

You need to determine downtime costs for individual users as well as complete systems. For example, you might want to find downtime costs for the following:

- Each workstation
- Each file server
- The entire building or campus network
- Each host gateway
- Each communications server or link

Determining costs isn't always easy. After assembling as much pertinent information as possible, such as staff costs (salaries, benefits, etc.), sales figures and overhead, you will probably have to resort to a technique widely used by experts of all stripes—the "educated guess." Using this technique, you estimate all costs for which you do not have actual data and add them to the equation.

When determining costs, keep one point in mind: averages don't count. You must look at worst-case situations. For an accounting firm, that might be the last two weeks of tax season. For a law firm, it might be the day before a big trial. For a Wall Street investment firm, it might be any time the stock markets are open. The worst case is different for every organization.

Costs will generally increase over time. As organizations "downsize" and move more critical applications to the LAN, the cost of downtime will increase at a greater rate than normal. You need to reassess these costs on a regular basis.

How Long and How Often Can You Afford to Be Down?

If you ask most LAN administrators how much downtime they can afford, the answer will usually be "none." In most cases, however, this is an unrealistic answer. First of all, eliminating all downtime is nearly impossible. Attempting to eliminate all downtime can also be extremely costly. In most cases, you should implement procedures and systems that guarantee that you will keep downtime within predefined parameters.

Table 1-1: Example Worksheet: Costs and Effects of Downtime

Component	Results (examples)	Cost/hr (examples)
File Server in Sales	No access to sales department files	$20,000
File Server in Engineering	No access to engineering files	10,000
Host Gateway	No access to host	$5,000
Workstation in Sales	Lost sales	$300
Workstation in Engineering	Lost productivity	$150
Wide Area Network Link	No access to branch office	$1,000
Remote Access Server	No access from the field, lost sales	Difficult to calculate
Network Cabling or Hubs	No access from workstation(s)	$50-$30,000

How do you determine what those parameters are? You need to look at the potential results of downtime for various LAN components. Table 1-1 is an example of one method of charting this information. It is somewhat simplistic, but it should get the idea across. You might use a similar method to look at the costs and chart effects of downtime for specific components of your system. Please note that this is for planning purposes only, to get a handle on costs. This is not information that you need to maintain.

Once you have looked at the potential results of downtime, start setting the parameters for maximum downtime and maximum downtime frequency (Table 1-2). Allowable downtime is the amount of downtime you can have without a major effect on the organization or incurring substantial losses.

Table 1-2: Example Worksheet: Allowable Downtime

Component	Maximum Downtime	Maximum Frequency of Downtime
File Server	4 hours	Once per month
Host Gateway	4 hours	Once per week
User Workstation	24 hours	Twice per year
Wide Area Link	24 hours	Once per month
Async Comm Server	4 hours	Twice per month

To set realistic parameters, you will need to talk to users and department managers as well as upper management. You will need their assistance in determining realistic parameters. You also need to reassess these parameters on a regular basis. As you increase reliance on the LAN, the maximum allowable downtime will get shorter. Once you have these parameters, you have a target for your disaster plan. Be aware, however, that these numbers are temporary. They will change over time, with the allowable duration and frequency going down.

The Goal: Minimum Downtime

Zero downtime, or at least zero *unplanned* downtime, is a goal many people feel they should strive for. Unfortunately, this goal is unattainable, or at least has been so far in the short history of computing. Setting an unattainable goal is counterproductive, as it sets up an impossible level of expectation and causes discouragement. The best you can do is *minimize* downtime.

As discussed in Chapter 2, minimizing downtime will require a lot of little steps, with the involvement of all concerned. If you take the right steps, each step can help limit your exposure to downtime but not eliminate its possibility. To put it another way, every step you take toward the goal of eliminating downtime can possibly take you part of the way there but not all the way there. The closer you come to attaining this goal the less overall effect each step will have. If you set unrealistic expectations, you set yourself (and your company) up for a disaster for which you are not prepared.

What Do You Need to Protect Against?

Disasters come in many forms, including:

- Hardware and software failure, including disk crashes, cabling problems, and operating system and application problems

- Human error, including accidental file deletions

- Sabotage, including viruses and vandalism

- Natural disasters, such as fire, flood, earthquake or hurricane

- Power-related problems

- Environmental contamination, including PCB and asbestos contamination

- Theft

Even if a particular disaster doesn't seem likely, could you recover if it occurred? For example, floods are not common in downtown Chicago, but one happened in 1992. Since you can't anticipate every possible disaster, you need to be prepared for the unexpected (Table 1-3).

Table 1-3: Possible Disasters and Effects

What Can Happen	Possible Effects	Prevention or Recovery
Cabling Problems	System unavailability, costly and time-consuming trouble-shooting	Structured cabling system, proper design, documentation, monitoring and diagnostic tools
Server or Host Disk Failure	System unavailability, data loss or corruption	Mirrored or duplexed drives, redundant array of inexpensive disks (RAID)
Server or Host Failure	System unavailability, data loss or corruption	Spare server, server mirroring, host redundancy
LAN Component Failure (NIC, Hub, etc.)	Full or partial system unavailability, data loss or corruption, costly and time-consuming troubleshooting	Spare components, trained support staff, proper test equipment and troubleshooting procedures
Network OS Failure or Bug	Full or partial system unavailability, data loss or corruption, costly and time-consuming troubleshooting	Current patches and fixes
Accidental File Deletion	Data loss	Effective data backup system, undelete utilities
Power Outage	System unavailability, data loss or corruption, hardware damage	UPS, backup generator
Power Defect	Data loss or corruption, hardware damage, costly and time-consuming troubleshooting	Proper power conditioning equipment
Lightning	Data loss or corruption, hardware damage	Network segmentation, LAN cable surge protection

Table 1-3: Possible Disasters and Effects (Continued)

What Can Happen	Possible Effects	Prevention or Recovery
Viruses	Full or partial system unavailability, data loss or corruption, costly and time-consuming troubleshooting	Up to date virus-checking and eradication software, proper data backup procedures, user education
Sabotage	Full or partial system unavailability, data loss or corruption, hardware or software damage, costly and time-consuming troubleshooting	Proper security, recovery plan, good user relations
Loss of Key Personnel	Inability to manage system or resolve problems	Cross-training and planning
Theft (Physical Property)	Unavailability of system or components	Proper physical security, equipment acquisition plan, easily available components
Theft (Data)	Lost competitive position, legal liability	Proper physical security, access control, data encryption
Natural Disaster	Loss of life, site unavailable, key personnel unavailable, no power, transportation	Off-site business resumption plan, cross-training
Miscellaneous Intermittent or Recurring Problems	Full or partial system unavailability, costly and time-consuming troubleshooting, data loss or corruption	Tracking occurances and correlating with other events, electrical power analysis, network monitoring, use of outside professionals

How Much Protection Do You Need?

With disaster protection, as with insurance, it is either impossible or cost-ineffective to protect yourself from every potential problem. You need to provide a reasonable amount of protection against downtime and data loss while making sure you can recover in a timely fashion when disaster strikes. As you attempt to move closer toward the goal of total elimination of downtime, two things will become apparent: each incremental step will be significantly more costly than the previous one, and each will provide a significantly smaller amount of protection.

In the final analysis, you can't completely prevent downtime, you can only minimize it. You must decide what steps will be cost-effective for your situation.

The Grand Plan, or One Step at a Time?

By their very nature LANs are uncontrollable and unpredictable. They will grow and change in ways that no one expects. This provides for a very flexible system that can respond quickly to changing needs, but this flexibility has a price: in most organizations, no one group or individual can keep track of or control everything that happens. Therefore, no one person or group can know everything required to implement an effective disaster plan for a large, complex LAN. Traditional, top-down IS management and control of a LAN disaster plan is next to impossible to achieve. This doesn't mean that effective LAN disaster plans can't be implemented; it just means that you may have to look beyond traditional methods and ideas to do it.

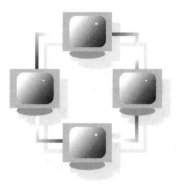

Planning the Plan

A s with any other well-laid plan, a number of steps are required to create an effective LAN disaster plan. This includes assessing potential risks, gathering information about your system and its uses and users, writing the plan, educating those involved about their roles and then testing the plan. Of course, periodic updates will also be required. It looks pretty straightforward, right? Unfortunately, this is usually not the case.

Why LAN Disaster Planning Is So Very Hard to Do

The key to the difficulty in building a LAN disaster plan lies in the difference in the structures of traditional data centers and LAN-based systems.

The traditional data center is highly structured, with tight controls placed over access, applications and usage. The data center is also separate from the rest of the organization as a whole, allowing it to be managed as a single, separate entity. The data center is usually structured in a strict hierarchical fashion, and as such lends itself to effective top-down management. New applications are usually added only after much thought and deliberation, and all system changes are planned well in advance.

LANs are different. They are not centrally managed, they connect multiple types of devices, often support hundreds of applications and are intertwined within the fabric of the organization. Control and management are often handled by many different individuals at different levels, in different departments or workgroups with different goals and viewpoints. New applications are often added to workgroup servers (or users' workstations) at a moment's notice, and system components, such as file servers, workstations and printers, are often added or changed without the knowledge of central IS. The users expect to control the LAN, or at least their portions of it. This is almost never true in the traditional data center.

The primary difference, however, is this: The data center is an information resource, while the LAN is the information highway. The LAN connects the user to many information resources located throughout (and sometimes outside) the organization. Data center disaster planning means protecting one large resource under the control of one group, where changes are controlled and well-planned. LAN disaster planning, however, means protecting multiple resources under the control of multiple groups and individuals, where change happens quickly without central control.

To use the terminology of the relatively new science of chaos, LANs are *dynamical*[1] *systems*, or systems that are in a constant state

---

[1]*Dynamical* in this context means *continuously active*.

of change. They are composed of so many interacting elements that they can be sensitive to even the smallest factors. Complex dynamical systems are also subject to the effects of feedback. When systems are affected by excessive *positive feedback*, revolutionary changes take place. For example, placing a microphone in front of a loudspeaker will amplify noise and static to the point that it creates a deafening screech. Systems that exhibit this kind of behavior are said to be *nonlinear*. In nonlinear systems, the slightest change in one area can affect the entire system in unexpected ways. When someone explodes in anger over some seemingly trivial event, engineers will often say something like "He went totally nonlinear!"

Because LAN-based systems are made up of so many different components, "going nonlinear" is not all that unusual an occurrence. For example, a cabling problem might not manifest itself until you add one more workstation and the system crashes completely. Changing a software driver for a LAN card at one station can create problems for everyone else if that driver is incompatible with the others on the network. This means that you can't be prepared for every contingency, and you have to be prepared for totally unexpected things to happen.

Because LANs are ever-growing, ever-changing, nonlinear dynamical systems, writing a comprehensive disaster plan that covers every component and contingency is difficult at best, impossible at worst. Before you have finished writing a comprehensive plan it will be obsolete. In most organizations, no one group or individual can keep track of or control everything that happens. Therefore, no one person or group can know everything required to implement an effective disaster plan for a large, complex LAN.

So, how can you build a comprehensive LAN disaster plan? The answer is simple: in all but the smallest organizations, you can't. You need to implement a number of smaller plans. This means that instead of a central IS group being responsible for all disaster planning, much of the responsibility must rest with those affected. If you have departmental LANs or servers, let the departments implement departmental plans. If you have a central IS group, let them take care of facilities under their control, and let them act as facilitators, coordinators and cheerleaders for everyone else.

If you are part of a central IS group, start the planning process for those systems and components for which you have direct responsibility. At the same time, begin finding ways to assist others in building plans for their systems or departments. You may not be able to exert top-down control, but if you do your job right you can create standards and guidelines that will be followed by others.

If you are a departmental or workgroup LAN manager, start working with your staff and users to create your own disaster plans. See if you can find ways to coordinate your planning with others, especially central IS.

If you are the manager of a LAN in a small company or an independent division of a large company, you are pretty much on your own. Work with your staff and users to create your plans.

Kaizen

One of the major underpinnings of the success of Japanese business is the concept or philosophy of *kaizen*, which means constant, continuous improvement over time involving everyone. Why mention *kaizen* in a book about LAN disaster planning? Because the traditional American approach to problem-solving is to make sweeping changes from the ground up. Terms like *business re-engineering, software re-engineering* and *project* usually refer to the idea of massive, top-to-bottom changes. This approach usually consists of one group of "experts" making decisions that affect everyone. This approach is also known as *The Grand Plan*. Given our premise that due to the diversity of LANs no one group can know everything, *The Grand Plan*, in terms of disaster planning, will be at best inadequate and at worst a dismal failure. This is not to say that central coordination is not helpful or needed, just that attempts at total top-down planning, a la the Soviet Union, will ultimately fail.

The *kaizen* approach, however, says make little changes and get feedback from everyone. In other words, make disaster prevention and recovery everyone's job. In their excellent book, *The Virtual Corporation*,[2] William H. Davidow and Michael S. Malone state:

> *One of the greatest strengths of kaizen is the speed with which it can incorporate the latest technological changes... One reason why a kaizen-driven company can do this so efficiently is that its entire work force is oriented toward locating new ideas and swiftly and effectively putting them to work. In essence, every employee becomes a management consultant.*

If no one person or group can build and maintain a disaster plan, then maybe the best approach is to let everyone do it! Unfortunately, this runs counter to standard business practices in many U.S. companies. It requires really listening to the concerns and ideas of everyone, from the CEO down to the lowest-paid shipping clerk. This means that the hierarchical structures that served business well when change was slow will need to be "flattened" to function in today's fast-paced, ever-changing business environment. The lines of communication need to be changed, making it easier for anyone to communicate with anyone else in the organization.

---

[2]William H. Davidow and Michael S. Malone, *The Virtual Corporation* (HarperCollins Publishers, 1992), p. 129. It is this author's opinion that this book should be required reading for anyone involved in computer or LAN systems management.

Although Davidow and Malone don't actually define a *virtual corporation*, they do describe it as follows:

> *To the outside observer, it will appear almost edgeless, with permeable and continuously changing interfaces between company, supplier, and customers. From inside the firm the view will be no less amorphous, with traditional offices, departments and operating divisions constantly reforming according to need.*[3]

What they are describing are organizations that can respond quickly to changing business needs. Since LAN-based systems are, in effect, *virtual computer systems* which change and grow quickly, we must adopt a similar approach to respond to the changing needs of the organization and users. In both the Japanese philosophy of *kaizen* and Davidow's and Malone's concept of the virtual corporation, trust in and participation of all concerned is key. In many organizations this will require major changes in attitudes. It will also require training and access to needed information for system managers and users alike. This approach can be summed up as follows:

An effective disaster prevention and recovery plan involves everyone. It is composed of a series of small steps, and is continuously tuned, tweaked and improved over time.

Who's Responsible for What?

If you are going to build a number of smaller plans, who is going to be responsible? One way to start is to see who has primary

---

[3]Davidow and Malone, *The Virtual Corporation*, p. 5

responsibility for the various parts of the LAN. For example, in many larger organizations, a central IS group is responsible for the physical network plant, including hubs, cabling, and so forth. That same group might be responsible for hardware repair and maintenance, centralized backup and overall system coordination. Workgroup administrators, however, might be responsible for those things that directly affect their users, such as server management, application maintenance and user account maintenance. In addition to the centralized backup handled by IS, the workgroup manager might be responsible for a secondary backup.

Looking at your organization you will probably see a similar structure, with some areas of overlapping responsibility (see Figure 2-1). This is also one way to structure your disaster plan. In our example, each workgroup manager and his or her staff is responsible for disaster prevention and recovery in that area, while IS is responsible for those areas that affect everyone. IS can also act as a backup to the workgroup staff, filling in where and when needed.

By creating smaller plans in this manner, it is easier to accommodate change as well as serve the needs of each department or workgroup.

On the downside, you need to be aware that with responsibility comes accountability. In our litigious American society, IS, LAN and department managers face an increasingly complex web of legal entanglements, and in many cases could be held civilly or criminally liable for breaches in security, loss of data, software piracy, theft of trade secrets or intellectual property, improper e-mail access, or just about anything else for which a hungry attorney decides to sue you or your company.

Figure 2-2: Overlapping Spheres of Responsibility

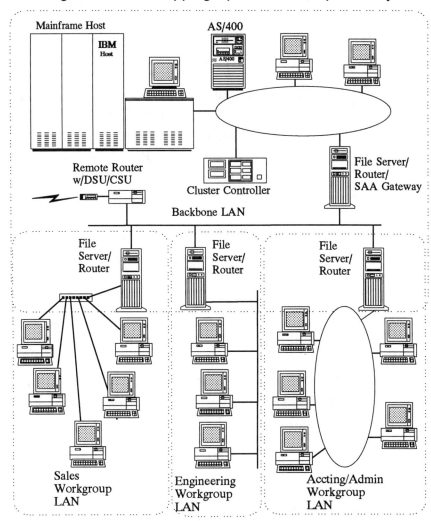

Personnel Issues

Burger King, headquartered in the South Miami area, was hit hard by Hurricane Andrew in 1992. CEO Barry Gibson brought this issue home. "Our business processes went on, but our people problems were massive. What do you do when 300 of your people are homeless?"[4] What good is a plan if there is no one to implement it?

Not all disasters are as massive as Hurricane Andrew, but in any regional disaster people are likely to be more concerned about the immediate welfare of their families than they are about getting the office up and running. The Pony Express hired unmarried orphans in an attempt to alleviate this problem, but that probably won't work very well today! Still, there are a number of things you can do:

- Cross-training is critical. More than one person in each group should have the knowledge and ability to perform each critical task.

- Extend your cross-training across workgroups. If staff from one group is not available, people from another workgroup or central IS should be able to fill in.

- When planning for disaster recovery, think in terms of job functions, not individuals. Depending on the type of disaster, some individuals may be unable or unwilling to get to the recovery site. In the case of a natural disaster, such as a hurricane or earthquake, roads and bridges could be knocked out, or, as noted above, people may need to take care of their families.

---

[4]*USA Today*, September 22, 1992

■   All written recovery plans and documentation should be readable and usable by nontechnical people. You should document even the most basic things. For example, documentation for restoring data from tape backup should cover such things as how to put a tape in the tape drive and, of course, how to turn the tape drive on.

Risk Assessment

What about formal risk assessment studies? By identifying potential problems, they can help with disaster prevention. They can also help focus planning efforts on types of disasters that are likely to happen and help justify disaster planning and prevention expenditures. There are two problems with them, however: they cost a lot of money, and they are not good indicators of the disasters that *will* happen. One IS manager said it best: "The disaster we planned for wasn't the one that happened."

For most of us, a massive terrorist bomb in the basement of the building which takes out communications links and closes the building for weeks would not be at the top of our list of possible risks. However, this is exactly what happened at the World Trade Center in New York in February 1993. The point here is that it is not the likelihood of a particular disaster that you need to plan for, but the effect. For example, planning for a hurricane in Des Moines, Iowa in the middle of the United States doesn't make a lot of sense, but planning for an office building being severely damaged, destroyed or otherwise inaccessible does make sense. The possibility of a particular cause may be low, but the possibility of the potential risk associated with that cause is very high. Giving too much credence to probable disasters can lull people into a false sense of security and make them ignore those disasters that are less probable. A good rule of thumb is:

Limit potential causes, but plan for possible effects.

Table 2-1 lists some potential risks and their possible causes.

Table 2-1: Risks and Their Possible Causes

Risk	Possible Causes
Building or Office Damaged, Destroyed or Otherwise Unavailable	Fire, flood, earthquake, hurricane, tornado, environmental contamination, bombing, severe damage to nearby building, sustained power outage
Full or Partial System Unavailability	All of the above, poor design, faulty installation, hardware failure, software failure, sabotage, cabling problems, human error, power problems, lightning, viruses, theft, remote communications links
Data Corruption or Unavailability	Poor design, faulty installation, hardware failure, software failure, data backup system failure, human error, viruses, sabotage, remote communications links
Unauthorized Access to Confidential Data	Poor design, poor security, human error, sabotage

How Much Does It Cost?

There are four types of costs that you need to calculate (or estimate): the cost of the effects of a disaster, the costs associated with disaster prevention measures, the costs associated with disaster recovery planning, and the costs associated with actual disaster recovery. These cost figures are important for the planning process and for selling the plan(s) to management and staff. Tables 2-2 through 2-5 (at the end of this chapter) are samples of the kind of cost information you may want to track.

Selling the Plan (To Everyone!)

Traditional disaster planning approaches discuss selling your disaster plan to management. Selling to management is important, but in today's down-sized, flattened (in terms of hierarchy) organizations, you will need the assistance of everyone. This means you will need to sell the concepts of disaster prevention and recovery to people at all levels in the organization. How do you do this?

In order to sell your disaster plan, or specific parts of it, you need to express yourself in terms the "buyer" will understand. In this case, the buyer is whomever you need to sell your disaster plan(s) to. In sales this is called finding the buyer's "hot button," which is an overwhelming reason for the customer to buy your product or service.

In his book about network interoperability, *Stacks* (Prentice Hall), Carl Malamud presented a revised version of the OSI model for data communications. In his model he compressed the familiar seven layers into four and then added three new ones on top: *Finance*, *Politics* and *Religion*. Reasons to buy can be technical (the bottom layers), political, financial or religious (Figure 2-2).

For example, saying to a CFO "We need to buy a $5,000 tape backup system so we can perform unattended backups" will usually be met with a blank stare, an automatic "no" or "we'll discuss it at the next budget meeting" (another way of saying "no"). However, saying "If we implement unattended backup with a $5,000 high-capacity tape drive we can save $7,800 the first year alone in salary and simplify the job of restoring data during an emergency" will probably be met with "Why aren't we doing this already?" In this case, the CFO's hot button is saving money (financial). Saying that you need to spend money is different from saying how much you will save.

You may have to explain the potential ramifications of the loss of your system or data differently to different people. While cost to the company and corporate liability issues may make an impression on corporate officers, they may have little impact on users. The possibility of office closures or layoffs, however, will often get the users' attention.

Figure 2-4: Carl Malamud's Revised OSI Model

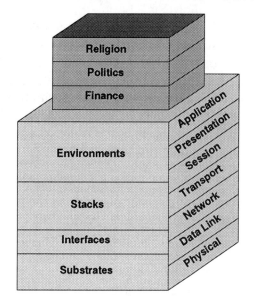

In organizations with mainframe computers, a common complaint by LAN administrators is that "All the money goes to support the mainframe and none of it comes to us. Management doesn't understand that all access to the mainframe is now done through the LAN!" Because mainframes cost a lot of money and PCs and LANs cost, by comparison, very little, management often uses cost to measure their relative importance. Part of your job is to sell management on the idea that cost and importance are separate issues.

Selling can be done both formally and informally. The traditional approach is to get all your facts and figures together, and then make a presentation to management. This is fine, but it is not enough. First, you should build support for your plans before a formal presentation. You will also need the support of those affected. Having a plan that is not understood and not wanted forced on people by management is a good way to guarantee that the plan will encounter considerable resistance and possibly even subtle (or not so subtle) forms of sabotage.

Support is built through cooperation with others and understanding their needs. If you do not have the people skills to do this, maybe you can enlist the aid of someone who does, or maybe you could (and probably should) learn the required skills. Support is also built by example. Demonstrating the strength of your approaches by implementing them on a small scale is an effective way of convincing others of their value. Disaster plans are built over time, and convincing an entire organization of their necessity and validity may also take time.

A word of caution here: Even if you think you have the best approach to disaster planning in the world, listen to others. There are probably things you have missed in your plans, and portions that may work for you may not work for others. Also, if it comes down to a confrontation with someone with an opposing view, bear in mind that an imperfect plan is usually better than none at all. Almost all plans are imperfect and need to be tweaked and modified over time.

Table 2-2: Sample Recovery Item Costs

Recovery Item	Possible Costs
Move to Business Recovery Site	$60,000-80,000 per week
Return to Office and Reintegrate Data	Cannot calculate w/o more info
Move to Long-Term Temporary Site	Cannot calculate w/o more info
Purchase New Computer and Network Equipment	800,000.00

Table 2-3: Sample Prevention Items

Prevention Item	Possible Costs	Benefits	Cost Benefits	Cost/Effects of Not Implementing
Survey, Test and Document Cabling System, Repair as Necessary	$2,000-10,000	Decrease or eliminate downtime due to cabling-related problems, reduce repair and troubleshooting time and costs	$8,500/yr (based on last year's estimated costs of downtime and repair)	Continued downtime and repair costs, potential for increased downtime
Document Backup and Restore Procedures	$500-1,500	Assure proper backup and restore procedures are followed	Difficult to calculate	Potential for serious data loss due to improper backup or restore
Inventory and Document System Hardware and Software	$3,000-5,000 first year, $1,500-2,500/yr thereafter	Decrease loss due to theft, decrease repair and maintenance time and costs	Unknown	Continued risk of theft, higher maintenance costs, possible legal liability due to software licensing problems
Install Duplexed External Drives on File Servers	$6,000-12,000 per file server	Decrease or eliminate potential downtime due to server hard disk failure	$10,000-30,000 per hour of downtime eliminated	Current single internal drives can take 1-3 days to replace and reinitialize
Purchase Spare File Server	$4,000 (when using external disk systems)	Keep downtime due to server failure to 10 minutes or less	$10,000-30,000 per hour of downtime eliminated	Current server configurations can take 1-3 days to repair and reinitialize

Table 2-4: Sample Possible Disasters

Possible Disaster	Possible Effects	Costs	Effects on Business	Prevention or Recovery
Earthquake or Major Building Fire	Severe damage or destruction of building	Not enough information to calculate	Temporary or permanent relocation	Off-site recovery plan
Fire in Main Wiring Closet	Loss of all network hubs, loss of communications links	$50,000 in equipment losses, estimated $75,000-150,000 in repair costs, plus downtime and/or relocation costs	Downtime, temporary relocation	Automatic extinguisher system, off-site recovery plan
File Server Crash	Loss of access to data and applications	$10,000-30,000 per hour downtime costs	Downtime	Duplexed external disk systems, spare server
Unauthorized Access to Product Design Information	Theft of designs, competitive advantages lost	Impossible to calculate, but potentially millions of dollars	Loss of income, loss of market share	Improved security measures
Virus Infection	Loss of data, downtime	$10,000-30,000 per hour downtime costs, data loss difficult to calculate	Downtime	Education, virus detection and eradication software and procedures

Table 2-5: Sample Recovery Planning Items

Recovery Plan-ning Item	Possible Costs	Benefits	Cost Benefits	Effects of Not Implementing
Written Off-Site Recovery Plans	$10,000-25,000	Improve chances of business recovery in a major disaster	Prevent major losses of thousands or millions of dollars	Loss of income, loss of clients, legal liability, possible loss of company
Periodic Updates	$2,000-10,000	Keep plans up to date	Prevent major losses of thousands or millions of dollars	Loss of income, loss of clients, legal liability, possible loss of company
Contract with Business Recovery Site Contractor	$2,000-6,000 per month	Improve chances of business recovery in a major disaster	Prevent major losses of thousands or millions of dollars	Loss of income, loss of clients, legal liability, possible loss of company
Telephone and On-Site Support Contract with LAN VAR	$300-1,000 per month	Improve chances of solving problems quickly	Prevent downtime at $75-300 per person per hour	Downtime, lost productiv-ity
Backup Communication Link with 2nd Vendor	$600 per month	Improve chances of reestablishing communications with field office quickly	difficult to calculate at this time	Lost sales, lost productiv-ity

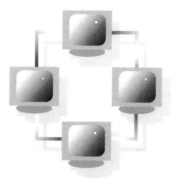

3

Documentation

*O*ne important tool for disaster prevention and recovery is good documentation. Proper documentation can prevent mistakes from happening and make sure that a recovery process goes smoothly. Manuals supplied with hardware and software are fine for what they are intended for, but they do not provide any information about your policies, procedures or configurations.

So, what kind of documentation do you need? Needs will vary from organization to organization, but in general the following list is appropriate:

■   General System Policies and Procedures

■   Hardware and Software Configurations

- User Basics

- Administrator Basics

- Troubleshooting and Problem Resolution

- Data Backup and Restoration Procedures

- Repair Procedures

- Service Provider and Warranty Information

- Business Recovery Plan

- Employee Address and Phone Lists

One big problem with documentation is maintenance. Many companies have spent thousands of dollars for staff or outside consultants to create documentation only to find that they had no effective mechanism for maintaining and updating it. Make sure when planning and designing your documentation that you have effective methods for maintenance.

Here are some tips to help make documentation easier:

- Be clear, concise and to the point. For example, two or three pages on basic backup or restore procedures are likely to be more effective than a detailed treatise that covers all contingencies. Use the KISS method: Keep It Simple and Straightforward.

- Write your documentation so that it can be read and used by a nontechnical person. When you know a system or process well, jargon and technobabble aren't a problem. But what if someone with less experience has to fill in during an emergency? What if you need to use your own documentation two years down the road when you have forgotten much of what you know now?

■ Don't use acronyms without defining them. Standard practice is to use the entire phrase once, followed by the acronym in parentheses. Example:

> *A local area network (LAN) is a high-speed communications system connecting various electronic components.*

In manuals that are not always read from cover to cover, it is a good idea to do this in each section that may be used separately.

■ Include a glossary of terms at the end of each document. Even two- or three-page documents can benefit from this.

■ Create modular documentation. If you break your documentation down into modules, maintenance is much easier. Also, you can often use documentation modules from one system, sometimes with minor modifications, for another system.

■ When possible, documentation should be created and maintained by people directly involved with the system(s) or procedure(s) being documented. This helps assure that those involved understand what they're documenting and eliminates the learning curve and time lag that are inevitable when third parties are involved.

■ Train those involved in the use of the tools they will be using for creating and maintaining documentation, and make sure those tools are easily available. (See *Creating and Maintaining Documentation* below.)

"IT'S A MEMO FROM SOFTWARE DOCUMENTATION. IT'S EITHER AN EXPLANATION OF HOW THE NEW SATELLITE COMMUNICATIONS NETWORK FUNCTIONS, OR DIRECTIONS FOR REPLACING BATTERIES IN THE SMOKE DETECTORS."

Have your documentation reviewed and tested by a third party who does not have extensive knowledge of the system or process being documented. This is the only way to find out what steps you forgot to include, or what is confusing or inaccurate.

■   When possible, document as you go. Creating your documentation as you install a new system, component or application is usually easier than going back to do it after the fact. When you go back after the fact, you usually have to relearn significant portions of the system or procedure being documented.

■   If you are documenting after the fact, document a piece at a time. Set up a schedule and a plan to document each component of your system. (See the next item.)

■   Make a list of things to be documented, then prioritize that list. Document the most important things first. If, for some reason, you can't document the most important things first, document the next most important items. In any case, document *something* that needs to be documented; then go back to the more important things when they can be done.

■   If you have multiple LANs, consistency between them means more reusable documentation. That consistency also makes cross-training easier, so that personnel from one system can more easily handle the problems of another in an emergency.

Creating and Maintaining Documentation

When creating documentation, simplicity is a virtue. If the documentation process is complex, difficult or overly time-consuming, it will not get done, or, if it is done initially, it will not be maintained. Specific individuals must have the responsibility for creating and maintaining documentation, and deadlines and maintenance schedules need to be established.

There are a number of tools that you can use for documentation, with various levels of capability, cost and complexity. Not all of them are appropriate for all situations, and no one of them will solve all your documentation problems.

When you are planning and creating documentation, think about how it is going to be maintained and who will do it. Even those with the best of intentions find that maintaining documentation becomes a low-priority task in the day-to-day rush. The more you can automate the process, the less time you will need to spend on it. When you are selecting the tools you will use for documentation, consider how difficult the tools are to use and how long and steep the learning curve will be. In most cases, you are better off using a less sophisticated documentation tool that you and your staff know well and can use easily than a very powerful tool that is difficult to use or will easily be forgotten.

Word Processors

Your word processor will probably be your primary tool for documentation. With it you can take output from other programs and utilities and put that output in a consistent, readable format. Using your word processor also allows you to easily add information manually and change or delete incorrect information.

Network Management Utilities

Many of the utilities that are included with your network operating system can be used for documentation. These utilities should be able to give you information about user and group accounts, security, access rights and other network information. Some utilities will generate reports; others will only display information on the screen. If the utility will only display screen information, you can still use it to create documentation. Here are two methods that you can use under DOS:

■   If the utility generates line-by-line screen output, you can redirect that output to a file or printer by using the DOS *redirect* function. This is done by typing the command at the command line followed by a right carat or *greater than* sign (>) followed by the redirection path. For example, if you want a list of active users of a Novell NetWare file server, as well as their node addresses, you can use the command USERLIST/A from a DOS workstation. To redirect that output to a disk file, you would use the following syntax:

```
USERLIST/A > (d:\path\filename)
```

where (d:\path\filename) is the drive letter, directory path and name of the file that you wish to create. If you want to append data to an existing file, use the following syntax:

```
USERLIST/A >> (d:\path\filename)
```

The double carats (>>) will append the new data to the named file if it exists, or create the file if it doesn't. If you want to send output to a printer instead of a file, substitute the printer or port designation (LST:, PRN:, LPT1:, etc.) for *(d:\path-\filename)*.

- If the utility displays information a screen at a time, the process is a little more difficult. You will have to use the PC's PrintScreen function and capture output to a file. If your network operating system doesn't provide the ability to capture to a file, there are public-domain and shareware utilities that do. These can be downloaded from bulletin boards or information services such as CompuServe. Some commercially available print spoolers will also provide this capability. If you are using NetWare, the CAPTURE command will let you reroute printer output to a disk file. The syntax would be:

```
CAPTURE L=1 NA TI=0 CR= (d:\path\filename)
```

where (d:\path\filename) is the drive letter or volume name, directory path and name of the file that you wish to create.

Using the above techniques, many of the utilities that come with your network can be used for creating documentation. For example, Novell NetWare's™ WHOAMI command can document each user's access rights on a network. By adding this command to a login script or batch file, you could periodically send the output to a file. (See *Other Utilities* later in this chapter.)

Network Reporting Utilities

A number of utilities are available that are specifically designed for reporting network information. Most of these, however, are specific to a particular network operating system (NOS). For example, LAN Support Group's *Bindview NCS*,™ Frye Computer System's *NetWare Management*,™ and Cheyenne Software's *Cheyenne Utilities*™ are specifically designed to report NetWare-specific information. To find out what utilities are available for your NOS, check ads and reviews in trade magazines, attend user group meetings, or utilize on-line services. For example, Banyan, Novell and Microsoft all maintain forums on CompuServe, a commercial on-line information service where users can share information. In addition, many user groups maintain electronic bulletin boards where this kind of information is often available.

Inventory Utilities

There are a number of utilities available that are designed to inventory hardware and software on DOS or Macintosh™ work-stations. Some of these, such as Brightwork's *LAN Automatic Inventory*,™ LAN Support Group's *Bindview NCS*, Magee Software's *Network HQ*™ and Horizon Technology's *LAN Auditor*,™ are designed to collect information across the network, while others, such as Tally System's *PC Census*,™ are more oriented to stand-alone PCs.

There are also other differences. They differ in what information they collect, what desktop workstations they work with and what network operating systems they support. (Because these utilities change frequently, we will not attempt to outline the capabilities of each one here.) Some are NetWare-specific, some inventory hardware only, some will inventory hardware and software and some will inventory both DOS and Macintosh workstations while some will only inventory DOS workstations. In almost every case, some information will have to be added manually. When looking at these utilities you may want to look at their reporting capabilities or at least their file formats. If a utility uses a common file format, such as DBF (dBASE), WKS (Lotus 123™) or Btrieve,™ you can use a report writer to generate custom reports (See *Report Writers* below).

On-Line Documentation

Although printed documentation is great, sometimes it is not at hand when needed. Another approach is electronic documentation. Electronic documentation can be stored on network file servers and made available to anyone who needs it. It is often easier to update and maintain than printed documentation, and it can usually be searched for particular words and phrases.

There are a couple of approaches that you can take to electronic documentation. One approach is to put your documentation into a format readable by your word processor and put the documentation files into a shared directory. Using a table of contents file or the long-name capabilities of some word processors would allow a user to find the appropriate file. Many word processors have the capability to search all the files in a directory for a particular word or phrase, so users could actually perform text searches. This method has the advantage of using tools you probably already have, so there is little or no additional software cost and no learning curve.

A more sophisticated approach is to use a text-indexing database. There are a number of these available, and one of the most popular is Folio Corporation's *Folio Views*,™ which allows you to access information by following a series of menus or by finding any word, group of words, or phrase. Information can be viewed, printed or exported to a file. The latest version of Views will import and export data in a number of word processing and graphics formats, and also provides some structured database capabilities.

Electronic documentation is not a replacement for printed documentation. In an emergency, it is often possible to access printed documentation but impossible to access an electronic version. This is especially true if there are network problems that prevent access to the documentation. You can, however, coordinate your paper and electronic documentation. Both approaches to electronic documentation described above allow you to create or update printed versions.

Report Writers

What if you have a utility that can collect needed information but can't output it in a format that you need? That's what report writers are for. Report writers will read data in one format and output it in another. Products such as Data Access Corporation's *FLEX/QL*™ or Concentric Data System's *R&R Report Writer*™ will let you generate queries and reports of data stored in various database and spreadsheet formats and then output that data to a printer or a disk file. The output can be formatted as text or put into another database format. Magic Software's *Magic*™ functions as both a report writer and a nonprocedural application generator. With Magic you can read from or write to another application's data files and also create related databases of other information.

Other Utilities

A lot of utilities are available to help you with the documentation process. For example, executing the TREE command from MS DOS 5 and above from the root directory of each volume can give you a visual picture of each volume's directory tree. Using ">" or ">>" as described above will let you send output to a printer or a file.

There are a number of shareware and public-domain utilities that can assist you in documentation. You can find these utilities by scouring on-line services such as CompuServe or user group bulletin boards.

For example, by using a timer utility such as XTree Corporation's TIMERUN[1] you can set up a routine to use network, DOS and shareware utilities to periodically update a file of user information. The following example shows how you might do this with Novell's NetWare:

1. Put the TIMERUN utility in a directory to which every user has read access, such as SYS:PUBLIC, or a shared utility directory, such as SYS:PUBLIC\UTILITY.

2. Create a directory for reports. Users must have READ, WRITE, CREATE and DELETE rights to this directory. In our example, we have created a directory under SYS:SYSTEM called REPORTS.

3. Add the following to your system login script at a point after mapping search paths and home directories. Make sure that you have search paths mapped to the PUBLIC and UTILITY directories.

```
DOS SET ID ="%LOGIN_NAME"
; Set a DOS environment variable for the user's login
; Name.
DOS SET UID="%USER_ID"
; Set a DOS environment variable for the NetWare user
; ID.
DOS SET ADDR="%P_STATION"
; Set a DOS environment variable for the physical
; station address.
DOS SET FULL="%FULL_NAME"
; Set a DOS environment variable for the user's full
; name.
```

---

[1] TIMERUN can be downloaded from Library 2 of the PCVENE forum on CompuServe as a compressed file named TIMERU.ZIP.

```
DOS SET NET="%NETWORK_ADDRESS%"
; Set a DOS environment variable for the network
; address.
#TIMERUN EVERY 30 COMMAND /C X:\PUBLIC\BATCH\REPORT²
/DATA=V:\MAIL\%USER_ID\³
; Run Microsoft's MSD utility every thirty days for each
; user to generate a report on system setup. (Note: This
; line has wrapped. There is a space between \REPORT and
; /DATA.)
```

4. Create a batch file named UREPORT.BAT in a directory mapped as a search path with the following commands:

```
@ECHO OFF
ECHO ......        Please wait a few minutes while the
ECHO ......        system performs some diagnostic tests.
CD V:\SYSTEM\REPORTS
; Change the directory of logical drive V to the reports
; directory.
MSD /P V:\SYSTEM\REPORTS\%ID%.RPT
; Run Microsoft's MSD diagnostic utility and send output
; to a file named with the user's login name in a
; special REPORTS directory under SYS:SYSTEM.
ECHO .                    >> K:\SYSTEM\REPORTS\%ID%.RPT
ECHO .                    >> K:\SYSTEM\REPORTS\%ID%.RPT
ECHO LOGIN NAME:  %ID%    >> K:\SYSTEM\REPORTS\%ID%.RPT
ECHO .                    >> K:\SYSTEM\REPORTS\%ID%.RPT
ECHO  FULL NAME:  %WPID%  >> K:\SYSTEM\REPORTS\%ID%.RPT
ECHO .                    >> K:\SYSTEM\REPORTS\%ID%.RPT
ECHO    USER ID:  %UID%   >> K:\SYSTEM\REPORTS\%ID%.RPT
ECHO .                    >> K:\SYSTEM\REPORTS\%ID%.RPT
ECHO    NETWORK:  %NET%   >> K:\SYSTEM\REPORTS\%ID%.RPT
ECHO .                    >> K:\SYSTEM\REPORTS\%ID%.RPT
; Append the user's login name, full name, NetWare ID
; and network address to the file.
SAVEUSER %ID%             >> K:\SYSTEM\REPORTS\%ID%.RPT
; Run Wolfgang Schreiber's SAVEUSER utility to document
; user information such as directory and file rights.
ECHO .                    >> K:\SYSTEM\REPORTS\%ID%.RPT
VER /R                    >> K:\SYSTEM\REPORTS\%ID%.RPT
; Run the DOS VER command with the /R option to report
; the DOS version and revision level.
ECHO .                    >> K:\SYSTEM\REPORTS\%ID%.RPT
ECHO    ==END OF REPORT== >> K:\SYSTEM\REPORTS\%ID%.RPT
CD V:\DOSAPPS
; Return drive V to its default directory.
ECHO ......        End of Report.  Thanks for your patience!
```

---

[2]In this login script, drive X is a search path that points to the SYS:PUBLIC\UTILITY directory.

[3]In this login script, drive V is a "dummy" that is reset for each application in batch files.

Every 30 days a new file for each user will be created in a REPORTS subdirectory under the SYS:SYSTEM directory. This file will be named with the user's login name and will contain information such as the user's login name, full name, user ID, network and station addresses, plus the information reported by several DOS and shareware utilities. MSD is a diagnostic and reporting utility that ships with Microsoft Windows™ and MS-DOS™ 6.0. SAVEUSER is a public domain utility by Wolfgang Schreiber that reports information about a NetWare user, including security information and directory and file rights. VER is a DOS utility that reports the version and revision level (/R) of DOS. Examples of the output of MSD are shown later in this chapter.

CMOS Utilities. What about CMOS setup parameters? Intel-processor-based PCs keep track of certain configuration information, such as drive, video and memory parameters, in battery-powered CMOS memory. If the battery goes dead, you lose that information. There are a couple of utilities that can help. MSD will report CMOS information to a printer or file. CMOSSAVE, a free-to-use program by Stephen V. Genusa (available from numerous BBSes), will create a CMOS image file that can be used by its companion, CMOSREST, to reset CMOS information.

What to Document

When asked the question, "What should I document?" it is easy to glibly respond, "Everything!" In the best of all possible worlds, this would be either easy to do or not required at all. In our world, however, documentation takes valuable time that can often be used for better purposes, both at the office and away from it. (Yes, some LAN administrators actually DO have lives away from the office!) Probably the best answer is, "Document those things that are required or helpful in problem resolution and disaster recovery." This means you not only need to look at what you are going to document, but to what degree you will carry the task of documentation. For example, it is extremely helpful, for purposes of troubleshooting and disaster recovery, to have your cabling system documented. That means the information you need, such as a cabling diagram, cable types and so on. It doesn't mean that you have to track the manufacturer, model, cost and location of every 35 cent modular connector! The point here is to make sure you have enough detail, but not too much. Gathering unnecessary detail wastes time, and the excess information will usually just get in the way.

Other aspects to consider are how quickly things change and if there is more than one way to get certain information. For example, certain network management utilities will let you build documentation concerning which user is connected to which hub port. Usually, however, this requires some level of manual intervention. If your system is relatively stable, this might be fine. If you experience a lot of moves, adds and changes, or if the cables often get moved from one hub port to another, maintaining this documentation might be overly time-consuming. If your cables are properly labeled and you have a decent cabling map, you might find that you will expend less time and energy overall by tracking that kind of information as needed by using your cable maps and labels.

What you need to document will vary with your situation. Outlined here are some of the common areas that should be documented.

Cabling

With today's star-wired cabling systems, cabling is one of the easiest parts of your network to document. Proper cabling documentation is one of the best ways to cut troubleshooting time. Unfortunately, most cabling systems are not properly documented. Here are some tips on cabling system documentation:

■ When installing new cabling, have it documented and labeled by the installers. Most installers will do this if required, but many will not volunteer to do so. There may be extra charges involved, but the cost should be significantly less than doing it after the fact.

■ If you must document your cabling system after the fact, a cable scanner such as the Microtest MT-350™ with the Office Locator Kit makes this much easier (Figure 3-1).

Figure 3-1: The Microtest MT350 scanner can map a cabling system by locating numbered Office Locator plugs that are plugged in to wall outlets.

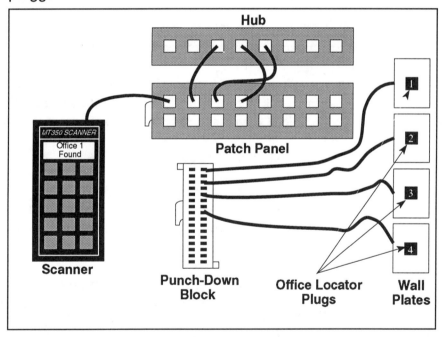

■ Label both ends of every through-the-wall cable and patch cable. Patch cables can have labels directly attached to each end. The Unitag™ from A 'n D Products is designed to do this quickly, neatly and easily (Figure 3-2). For through-the-wall cables, label the port on the wall plate at the client end and the patch panel port in the wiring closet. End-to-end labeling, such as labeling a PC and a hub port in the wiring closet, will not work in the long run, since every move will require relabeling.

Figure 3-2: A 'n D Unitag

■   Create and use a standard identification and naming scheme. Put as much pertinent information on the label as possible, such as cable ID, type and length. For example:

```
#12345 EIA568B 25Ft.
```

■   Use an electronic labeler such as the Brother P-Touch.™ These create easy-to-read labels with adhesive backs that are easy to apply. The more sophisticated models will even print bar codes for inventory tracking.

■   Create a maintainable map of your hard-wired or through-the-wall cabling. There are several ways to approach this:

   ■   Buy a commercial program designed for this purpose. There are several of these available, but they are expensive and usually have long learning curves.

- If you can obtain a blueprint of your office or building in electronic format and have a computer-aided design (CAD) program available, you can use the CAD program to maintain the wiring map. Here again, high cost and a long learning curve may be an issue.

- Use a drawing package to create simple diagrams. This approach will not be as accurate as the above methods, but it will usually cost less and have a shorter learning curve. *VISIO*™ from Shapeware is primarily a flow-charting program, but it lends itself well to this task (see Figure 3-3). A library of drag-and-drop network and computer images is included with the product, and a package of additional network images is available as an add-on.

Figure 3-3: Sample VISIO Drawing

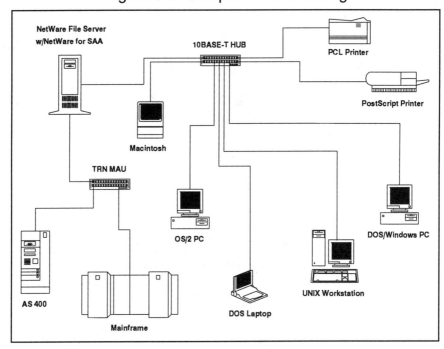

■   Even a simple text file listing the endpoints of each cable
     is better than nothing at all. This is the easiest approach,
     costs less than the alternatives and has the shortest learning
     curve. In terms of maintainability, this may be the best
     approach in many cases since almost anyone can maintain
     the document. It will not, however, be as easy to use for
     troubleshooting as the other approaches listed above.

Don't try to maintain end-to-end mapping (i.e. workstation to
hub port, including patch cables) in your document. If you do, every
minor change will require updating the cabling map.

Documentation Examples

In this section we will provide some examples of documentation
methods. The examples may not be exactly right for your systems,
but hopefully they will point you in the right direction.

A General System Manual

The following outline is for a general system manual designed
for use by LAN administrators and support staff. The system manual
should be easily available to anyone responsible for system
management or maintenance.

1. Introduction
    a. Guide to the manual
    b. System overview
    c. Roles and responsibilities of staff (users, LAN
        administrators, tech support, IS)
2. System components and basic setup
    a. Workstations
    b. File server(s)
    c. LAN cabling system
    d. Communications servers and modems

   e. Bridges and routers
   f. Printers
  3. Using the system
   a. Workstation operation
   b. Logging in/out
   c. The system menu (or GUI)
   d. Printing
   e. Basic file management
  4. System management
   a. File server startup and shutdown
   b. Overview of administrator utilities
   c. Standard directory structure
   d. Standard access rights and security structure
   e. User and group maintenance
   f. Application installation and maintenance
   g. Menu and user interface maintenance
   h. Protecting information
    i. Data security
    ii. Software licensing and protection
    iii. Requirements for backup
    iv. Use and abuse of passwords
    v. Host access
    vi. Storage of sensitive data on diskette or printout
   i. Backing up and restoring data
    i. Backing up data
     (1) Backup schedules
     (2) Standard backup procedures
     (3) Unscheduled backups
     (4) Tape storage
     (5) Off-site storage procedures
     (6) Backup system testing
     (7) Maintaining the tape library
    ii. Restoring data
     (1) Locating the correct tape and saveset
     (2) Restoring a single file or directory
     (3) Restoring a volume or file server

5. User support
   a. Training
   b. Available documentation
6. Troubleshooting and maintenance
   a. Basic troubleshooting procedures
   b. Using the troubleshooting database
   c. Standard repair procedures
   d. Support resources

A User Manual

The following outline is for a user manual. Much of it is taken from the system manual. Each user should have a copy of this manual.

1. Introduction
   a. Guide to the manual
   b. System overview
   i. Responsibilities of system users
   c. Protecting information
      i. Data security
      ii. Software licensing and protection
      iii. Use and abuse of passwords
      iv. Host access
      v. Storage of sensitive data on diskette or printout
2. Using the system
   a. Workstation operation
   b. Logging in/out
   c. The system menu (or GUI)
   d. Printing
   e. Basic file management
   f. Recovering lost data
   g. Training
   h. Available documentation
3. Trouble reporting and resolution

Server Documentation

Each network file server, communications server, host or other server should be fully documented, and that documentation should be put in a binder that is kept within easy reach of that file server. The information should include:

1. Brand, model, bus type, processor type and speed, memory on motherboard, BIOS date and supplier, keyboard type, I/O and video adapters on the motherboard, serial port UART type, any interrupts, I/O ports, base memory addresses or DMA channels used, motherboard switch and jumper settings
2. Expansion cards by slot
   a. Card make, model and serial number
   b. Any interrupts, I/O ports, base memory addresses or DMA channels used
   c. Revision, BIOS version, BIOS date, microcode version, microcode date, switch settings, software settings and serial port UART type, if applicable
   d. Drivers required
3. Internal hard disks
   a. Drive make and model
   b. Drive type in CMOS drive table, if applicable
   c. Number of partitions
   d. Partition OS
   e. Number of cylinders, heads and sectors per track
   f. Size
   g. Controller/host adapter make, model and type
   h. SCSI address(es), if applicable
   i. Disk channel or adapter, if applicable
4. External hard disks
   a. Drive make and model
   b. Drive type in CMOS drive table, if applicable
   c. Number of partitions
   d. Partition OS
   e. Number of cylinders, heads and sectors per track

        f.   Size

        g.   Controller/host adapter make model and type

        h.   SCSI address(es), if applicable

        i.   Disk channel or adapter, if applicable

5.   Floppy Disks

        a.   Location (1 or 2)

        b.   Size and capacity

6.   Other information

        a.   Memory size and type, including expansion card memory

        b.   IRQ, I/O port, base memory address and DMA channel usage

        c.   Printout of CMOS setup parameters

7.   Printouts of all startup files, such as AUTOEXEC.BAT, CONFIG.SYS files, and files such as NetWare's START-UP.NCF and AUTOEXEC.NCF

In addition to the above information, appropriate hardware and software manuals, including manuals for all interface cards, should be kept at the file server as well. The server manual should also contain diskettes with any files needed for rebuilding or maintaining that file server.

CMOS setup parameters can be printed by attaching a printer to your server, running the CMOS setup utility (the server will have to be shut down to do this), then using the <PrintScreen> key to print each setup screen.

The following is an abbreviated example of server documentation created using Microsoft's MSD. The file server must be booted under DOS to run this utility. After gathering the basics with MSD, additional information (marked with asterisks) was added by hand using a text editor.

System Board. In addition the information supplied by MSD, the system board information should include any switch and jumper settings.

```
--------------------- Summary Information ----------------------
                  Computer: Hauppauge/Award, 486DX
                    Memory: 640K, 15360K Ext
                     Video: VGA, Western Digit
                   Network: No Network
                OS Version: Non MS-DOS 3.31
                     Mouse: No Mouse Installed
            Other Adapters:
               Disk Drives: A: B: C:
                 LPT Ports: 1
                 COM Ports: 2

-------------------------- Computer ----------------------------
             Computer Name: Hauppauge
         BIOS Manufacturer: Award
              BIOS Version: 486 Modular BIOS v4.10.
             BIOS Category: IBM PC/AT
             BIOS ID Bytes: FC 01 00
                 BIOS Date: 05/14/91
                 Processor: 486DX
          Math Coprocessor: Internal
                  Keyboard: Enhanced
                  Bus Type: EISA
            DMA Controller: Yes
              Cascaded IRQ2: Yes
         BIOS Data Segment: None

--------------------------- Memory -----------------------------
Legend: Available " " RAM "##" ROM "RR"  Possibly Available ".."
  EMS Page Frame "PP"
1024K FC00 RRRRRRRRRRRRRRRR FFFF  Conventional Memory
      F800 RRRRRRRRRRRRRRRR FBFF            Total: 640K
      F400 RRRRRRRRRRRRRRRR F7FF        Available: 571K
 960K F000 RRRRRRRRRRRRRRRR F3FF                    585136 bytes
      EC00                  EFFF
      E800                  EBFF  Extended Memory
      E400                  E7FF            Total: 15360K
 896K E000                  E3FF
      DC00                  DFFF
      D800 ################ DBFF
      D400                  D7FF
 832K D000                  D3FF
      CC00 RRRRRR..         CFFF
      C800                  CBFF
      C400 RRRRRRRR........ C7FF
 768K C000 RRRRRRRRRRRRRRRR C3FF
      BC00 ################ BFFF
      B800 ################ BBFF
      B400                  B7FF
 704K B000                  B3FF
      AC00                  AFFF
      A800                  ABFF
      A400                  A7FF
 640K A000                  A3FF
```

```
MAIN BOARD INFORMATION------------------------------------------*
   SWITCH AND JUMPER SETTINGS

JP1 i860 Timer Int.              Upper (1-2)=30.8955 mSec
                                 Lower (2-3)=61-7911 mSec

                                 Setting=Upper (1-2)
```

```
    ┌─────────┐
    │  ┌───┐  │
    │  │ ■ │ 1│
    │  │   │  │
    │  │ ■ │ 2│
    │  │   │  │
    │  │ ■ │ 3│
    │  └───┘  │
    └─────────┘
```

```
JP 4 COM1/COM3 Select            Left (1-2)=Port A is COM1
                                 Right=(2-3)Port A is COM3
                                 Removed=Port A is Disabled

                                 Setting=Left (1-2)
```

```
    ┌──────────────┐
    │ ┌──────────┐ │
    │ │ ■   ■   ■│ │
    │ └──────────┘ │
    └──────────────┘
      1   2   3
```

```
JP 5 COM1/COM3 Interrupt         Installed=Int. (IRQ4) Enabled
                                 Removed= Int. (IRQ4) Disabled

                                 Setting=Installed
```

```
    ┌─────────┐
    │  ┌───┐  │
    │  │ ■ │  │
    │  │   │  │
    │  │ ■ │  │
    │  └───┘  │
    └─────────┘
```

```
JP 6 COM2/COM4 Select            Left (1-2)=Port B is COM2
                                 Right (2-3)=Port B is COM4
                                 Removed=Port B is Disabled

                                 Setting=Left (1-2)
```

```
    ┌──────────────┐
    │ ┌──────────┐ │
    │ │ ■   ■   ■│ │
    │ └──────────┘ │
    └──────────────┘
      1   2   3
```

```
JP 7 COM2/COM4 Interrupt         Installed=Int. (IRQ3) Enabled
                                 Removed= Int. (IRQ3) Disabled

                                 Setting=Installed
```

```
    ┌─────────┐
    │  ┌───┐  │
    │  │ ■ │  │
    │  │   │  │
    │  │ ■ │  │
    │  └───┘  │
    └─────────┘
```

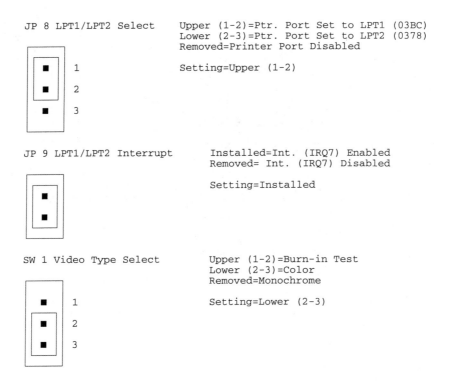

```
JP 8 LPT1/LPT2 Select          Upper (1-2)=Ptr. Port Set to LPT1 (03BC)
                               Lower (2-3)=Ptr. Port Set to LPT2 (0378)
                               Removed=Printer Port Disabled

              1                Setting=Upper (1-2)

              2

              3


JP 9 LPT1/LPT2 Interrupt       Installed=Int. (IRQ7) Enabled
                               Removed= Int. (IRQ7) Disabled

                               Setting=Installed




SW 1 Video Type Select         Upper (1-2)=Burn-in Test
                               Lower (2-3)=Color
                               Removed=Monochrome

              1                Setting=Lower (2-3)

              2

              3
```

Expansion Card Information. This section should include information on each card in the system, including slot, switch and jumper settings and EISA or MicroChannel setup information.

```
EXPANSION CARD INFORMATION-------------------------------------*

  Slot 1  SMC Elite 32T Ethernet Card
             Node Address 00800F661424
             Revision B
             Driver Version 1.42

  Slot 2 Paradise VGA card

  Slot 3 Empty

  Slot 4  Bus Logic BT542B SCSI Host Adapter
             Revision E
             BIOS Version 2.36
             Microcode Version 2.14
```

SW 1   1,2,3 = SCSI ID   Setting (ID 7) = 1,2,3 On
            4 = SCSI Parity   Setting (Enabled) = On
            5 = SCSI Auto-Sense   Setting (Enabled) = On
            6 = Sync Negotiation   Setting (Disabled) = On
            7,8 = DMA Channel   Setting (DMA 5 = 7,8 On

```
          ┌─────────────────────────┐   OFF
          │ ▪  ▪  ▪  ▪  ▪  ▪  ▪  ▪ │
          │ ■  ■  ■  ■  ■  ■  ■  ■ │   ON
          └─────────────────────────┘
            1  2  3  4  5  6  7  8
```

SW 2 1,2,3 = I/O Address   Setting (330-333h) = On
      4,5 = Host BIOS Addr.   Setting (Disabled) =4 On, 5 Off
      6,7,8 = Host IRQ Req.   Setting (IRQ 11) = 6,7,8 On

```
          ┌─────────────────────────┐   OFF
          │ ▪  ▪  ▪  ▪  ■  ▪  ▪  ▪ │
          │ ■  ■  ■  ■     ■  ■  ■ │   ON
          └─────────────────────────┘
            1  2  3  4  5  6  7  8
```

W11 and W13   Transfer Speed   Settings = Open
        Note: These must always be open

```
          ┌───────────┐
          │  ■   ■   │  13
          │          │
          │  ■   ■   │  11
          └───────────┘
```

W14,W15 and W16
14   Floppy Primary/Secondary I/O Setting = Open
            Note: This must always be open
15, 16   Floppy Disk Ctrlr   Setting (Disabled) = 15,16 Open

```
          ┌─────────────┐
          │  ■   ■   ■ │
          │            │
          │  ■   ■   ■ │
          └─────────────┘
           14  15  16
```

W17 I/O Channel Ready   Setting (Disabled) = A-B Jumpered

```
          ┌─────────┐
          │   ■    │  A
          │   ■    │  B
          │        │
          │   ■    │  C
          └─────────┘
```

```
W3-W8      Host IRQ Req.  Setting (IRQ 11 = W6
```

```
┌─────────────────────────┐
│  ■  ■  ■  ┌─┐  ■  ■     │
│           │■│           │
│  ■  ■  ■  │■│  ■  ■     │
│           └─┘           │
└─────────────────────────┘
```
```
    W3 W4 W5 W6 W7 W8
```

Slot 5 Empty

Slot 6 Everex MFM Disk Controller

Slot 7 Empty

Slot 8 Empty

Disk Drives. MSD will return information on drives that use the server's BIOS only. Information about other drives will need to be entered by hand.

```
----------------------- Disk Drives ---------------------------
Drive  Type                                 Free Space  Total Size
-----  ----------------------------------   ----------  ----------
  A:   Floppy Drive, 5.25" 1.2M
           80 Cylinders, 2 Heads
           512 Bytes/Sector, 15 Sectors/Track
  B:   Floppy Drive, 3.5" 1.44M
           80 Cylinders, 2 Heads
           512 Bytes/Sector, 18 Sectors/Track
  C:   Fixed Disk, CMOS Type 25                 69M         76M
           1023 Cylinders, 9 Heads
           512 Bytes/Sector, 17 Sectors/Track
                       Drive Type: Seagate ST 4096*
                       Partitions: 1*
                    Partition 1 OS: DR DOS 6.0*
            Controller/Host Adapter: Everex MFM w/Floppy Ctrlr*

NetWare Drive 0        Drive Type: Fujitsu M2266SA*
                       Partitions: 1*
                    Partition 1 OS: NetWare 3.11*
                         Cylinders: 1658*
                             Heads: 15*
                 Sectors Per Track: *
                              Size: 1023 MB*
                    CMOS Drive Type: 0*
            Controller/Host Adapter: Bus Logic 742 B*
                          Driver(s): ADIC DCB3200.DSK*
                                     ADIC DCBASPI.DSK*

NetWare Drive 0 -Fujitsu M2266SA - Switch and Jumper Settings --*
CN9
      1-2 Diagnostic                   Setting (Disabled) = Shorted
      5-6 Read-Ahead Caching    Setting (Enabled) = Shorted
      7-8 SCSI Time Monitoring      Setting (Enabled) = Shorted
      SCSI ID   Setting (0) = 9-10, 11-12, 13-14 Open
```

```
CNH2
     1-2  SCSI Level                     Setting (SCSI-2) = Shorted
     3-4  SAVE DATA POINTER         Setting (Issued) = Shorted
     5-6  Check Error Condition     Setting (Not Posted) = Shorted
     7-8  PER Default Mode          Setting (0) = Shorted
     9-10 Motor Start Mode          Setting (Immed. Start) = Shorted
     11-12 SCSI Bus Parity          Setting (Par. Chk Executed) =
Shorted
     13-14 Synch Mode Transfer      Setting (.096-4.8 MB/sec) =
Shorted
     15-16 Sync Mode Trans Req      Setting (Init. by Drive) = Shorted

CNH1

     1-2  LED Display               Setting (Drive Active) = Shorted
     11-12 Unit Attn                Setting (Check Cond.) = Shorted
     SCSI Time Monitoring and Retry Count
          Setting (Unlimited ACK wait time, 250ms Selection monitor-
          ing time, 128 retries) - 13-14 Shorted, 15-16 Shorted

Terminator Removed
```

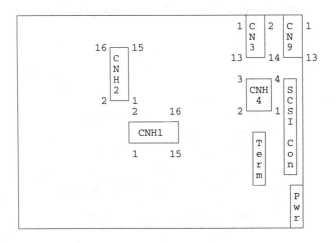

Logical System Data. Logical system includes COM port assignments, IRQs, DMA channels, RAM addresses and so on. This information can be important when attempting to troubleshoot server problems.

```
-------------------------- LPT Ports ----------------------------

              Port     On     Paper    I/O     Time
     Port   Address   Line     Out    Error    Out     Busy    ACK
     -----  -------   ----    -----   -----    ----    ----    ---
     LPT1:   03BCH     Yes     Yes      No      No      Yes     No
     LPT2:    -         -       -        -       -       -       -
     LPT3:    -         -       -        -       -       -       -
```

```
------------------------- COM Ports --------------------------

                          COM1:     COM2:     COM3:     COM4:
                          -----     -----     -----     -----
    Port Address          03F8H     02F8H      N/A       N/A
    Baud Rate             2400      2400
    Parity                None      None
    Data Bits               8         8
    Stop Bits               1         1
    Carrier Detect (CD)    No        No
    Ring Indicator (RI)    No        No
    Data Set Ready (DSR)   No        No
    Clear To Send (CTS)    No        No
    UART Chip Used        8250      8250

------------------------- IRQ Status -------------------------

IRQ  Address    Description        Detected         Handled By
---  --------   ---------------    --------------   ------------
  0  F000:FEA5  Timer Click        Yes              BIOS
  1  F000:E987  Keyboard           Yes              BIOS
  2  F000:EF6F  Second 8259A       Yes              BIOS
  3  F000:EF6F  COM2: COM4:        COM2:            BIOS
  4  F000:EF6F  COM1: COM3:        COM1:            BIOS
  5  F000:EF6F  SMC Elite 32T LAN Card*
  6  F000:EF57  Floppy Disk        Yes              BIOS
  7  F000:EF6F  LPT1:              Yes              BIOS
  8  F000:4093  Real-Time Clock    Yes              BIOS
  9  F000:ECF3  Redirected IRQ2    Yes              BIOS
 10  F000:EF6F  (Reserved)                          BIOS
 11  F000:EF6F  Bus Logic BT542B SCSI Host Adapter*
 12  F000:EF6F  (Reserved)                          BIOS
 13  F000:F0FC  Math Coprocessor   Yes              BIOS
 14  F000:ED00  Fixed Disk         Yes              BIOS
 15  F000:EF6F  (Reserved)                          BIOS

MEMORY ADDRESSES----------------------------------------------*

  Address     Size (Bytes)     Device*
  -----------------------------------------------------------*
  D0000       16KB             SMC Elite Ethernet Card*

DMA CHANNELS--------------------------------------------------*

  DMA Channel                  Device  *
  -----------------------------------------------------------*
  5                            Bus Logic BT542B SCSI Host Adapter*
```

Startup Files. Startup files include AUTOEXEC.BAT, CONFIG.SYS and startup files specific to your server OS (in this example, NetWare's STARTUP.NCF and AUTOEXEC.NCF). If possible, annotate the startup files themselves. (With some DOS versions, comments in CONFIG.SYS will generate error messages but will not affect the execution of the file.)

```
---------------------- C:\AUTOEXEC.BAT -------------------------
@ECHO OFF
PATH=C:\;C:\DRDOS
PROMPT [SONOMA DOS PARTITION] $P$G
DELAY /05 Start Server Sonoma?    (Y/N)
; Execute DELAY.COM to allow the operator to break out of the
; standard startup routine before the server operating system
; loads.
if errorlevel 2 goto SKIP
if errorlevel 1 goto SERVER
if errorlevel 0 goto SERVER
; These errorlevels are set by DELAY.COM.
:SERVER
C:
CD\NET311
SERVER
; Load the server operating system.
:SKIP


---------------------- C:\CONFIG.SYS -------------------------
SHELL=C:\COMMAND.COM C:\ /P /E:512
BREAK=ON
BUFFERS=15
FILES=20
FCBS=4,4
FASTOPEN=512
LASTDRIVE=E
HISTORY=ON, 256, OFF, OFF, OFF
COUNTRY=001,,C:\DRDOS\COUNTRY.SYS


STARTUP.NCF--------------------------------------------------------*
# Use a pound sign (#) before each comment line. Use a semicolon
# (;) to temporarily remove a command from the file.

LOAD DCB3200 PORT=330 INT=B DMA=5
# Load the driver for the ADIC-supplied BusLogic BT-542 SCSI host
# adapter.

LOAD DCBASPI
# Load the ASPI interface for the SCSI driver.

LOAD MAC
# Load the Macintosh Name Space.

SET MINIMUM PACKET RECEIVE BUFFERS=100
# Set the minimum number of buffers for incoming packets waiting to
# be processed to 100.

SET MAXIMUM PHYSICAL RECEIVE PACKET SIZE=4202
# Set the maximum packet size to accommodate 4KB packets.


AUTOEXEC.NCF--------------------------------------------------------*
# Use a pound sign (#) before each comment line. Use a semicolon
# (;) to temporarily remove a command from the file.

FILE SERVER NAME SONOMA
# Name the file server.
```

```
IPX INTERNAL NET 105
# Set a unique internal IPX network address.

SET TIMEZONE PST8
# Set the time zone for Pacific Standard Time, 8 hours after
# Greenwich Mean Time.

SET MAXIMUM ALLOC SHORT TERM MEMORY=3000000
# Increase the maximum amount of ALLOC SHORT TERM MEMORY from the
# default of 2,000,000 bytes to 3,000,000 bytes.

SET MAXIMUM PACKET RECEIVE BUFFERS=200
# Increase the maximum number of packet receive buffers from
# the default of 100 to 200.

SET ALLOW UNENCRYPTED PASSWORDS = ON
# Allow devices that cannot encrypt passwords access this file
# server.

LOAD SMCE32 PORT=1810 FRAME=ETHERNET_802.3 NAME=E8023NET
# Load the LAN driver for the SMC Elite 32T card, set the correct
# parameters for the card, install frame type ETHERNET_802.3, then
# name this configuration E8023NET. 802.3 is the default frame type
# for NetWare 3.11 and below.

BIND IPX TO E8023NET NET=101
# Bind the IPX protocol to E8023NET and assign network address 101.
# This must be consistent with the addresses that other file
# servers assign to this network using this frame type.

LOAD SMCE32 PORT=1810 FRAME=ETHERNET_802.2 NAME=E8022NET
# Reload the SMC Elite 32T driver and install frame type
# ETHERNET_802.2, then name this configuration E8022NET. 802.2
# is the default frame type for NetWare versions above 3.11.

BIND IPX TO E8022NET NET=8022
# Bind the IPX protocol to E8022NET and assign network address
# 8022. This must be consistent with the addresses that other file
# servers assign to this network using this frame type.

LOAD SMCE32 PORT=1810 FRAME=ETHERNET_II NAME=EIINET
# Reload the SMC driver and install frame type ETHERNET_II, then
# name this configuration EIINET. ETHERNET_II is the default frame
# type for TCP/IP.

LOAD TCPIP
# Load the TCP/IP protocol module.

LOAD SNMPLOG
# Load the SNMP error logging module.

BIND IP TO EIINET ADDR=1.0.0.3
# Bind the IP protocol to EIINET and assign IP address 1.0.0.3.

LOAD APPLETLK NET=50000 ZONE={"ADMIN"}
# Load the AppleTalk communications protocol and assign an internal
# file server zone and net address.

LOAD SMCE32 PORT=1810 FRAME=ETHERNET_SNAP NAME=ETALK2
# Reload the SMC driver and install frame type ETHERNET_SNAP, then
# name this configuration ETalk2. ETHERNET_SNAP is the default
# frame type for AppleTalk Phase 2.
```

```
BIND APPLETLK ETALK2 NET=1-5 ZONE={"SALES","SHIPPING","ACCTING"}
# Bind the AppleTalk protocol to the SMC driver, assign a network
# address range of 1-5, then assign zones.

LOAD AFP
# Load the AppleTalk Filing Protocol

LOAD ATPS
#Load AppleTalk print services

BSTART
# Start BTRIEVE with BSTART.NCF

RLOAD
# Execute the RLOAD.NCF file which loads the remote console support
# module (REMOTE.NLM) and the SPX support for the remote console
# (RSPX.NLM). Using a separate NCF file hides the remote console
# password.

LOAD MONITOR -P
# Load the monitor utility with the -P parameter. (-P displays
# processor utilization statistics.) Monitor is loaded last because
# it has a screen blanker. If Monitor is not the active console
# screen the screen blanker does not function.
```

Workstation Documentation

Each network workstation should be documented, and that documentation should be kept within easy reach of that workstation as well as in a central location accessible to the LAN administrator and support staff. The information should include:

1. Brand, model, bus type, processor type and speed, memory on motherboard, BIOS date and supplier, keyboard type, I/O and video adapters on the motherboard, serial port UART type, any interrupts, I/O ports, base memory addresses or DMA channels used, motherboard switch and jumper settings
2. Expansion cards by slot
   a. Card make, model and serial number
   b. Any interrupts, I/O ports, base memory addresses or DMA channels used
   c. Revision, BIOS version, BIOS date, microcode version, microcode date, switch settings, software settings and serial port UART type, if applicable
   d. Drivers required

3. Hard disks
   a. Drive make and model
   b. Drive type in CMOS drive table, if applicable
   c. Number of partitions
   d. Partition OS
   e. Number of cylinders, heads and sectors per track
   f. Size
   g. Controller/host adapter make model and type
   h. SCSI address(es), if applicable
   i. Disk channel or adapter, if applicable
4. Floppy disks
   a. Location (1 or 2)
   b. Size and capacity
5. External peripherals
   a. Make and model
   b. Controller/host adapter make model and type, if applicable
   c. SCSI address(es), if applicable
6. AUTOEXEC.BAT and CONFIG.SYS files
7. Local applications
   a. Application name
   b. Serial number and license information
   c. Configuration information
8. Other information
   a. Memory size and type, including expansion card memory
   b. IRQ, I/O port, base memory address and DMA channel usage
   c. Printout of CMOS setup parameters
   d. Drivers and memory managers

In addition to the above information, appropriate hardware and software manuals, including manuals for all interface cards as well as any required special software, should be available in a central location that is easily accessible. Copies should also be kept off-site, accessible in case of emergency.

The following is an example of DOS workstation documentation created using MSD, SAVEUSER and VER.

```
--------------------- Summary Information -----------------------
                    Computer: Compaq/Compaq, 80386
                      Memory: 639K, 11264K Ext
                       Video: VGA, Compaq
                     Network: Novell, Shell 3.26.00
                  OS Version: MS-DOS 5.00
                       Mouse: InPort Mouse
              Other Adapters:
                 Disk Drives: A: B: C: F: G: K: U: V:
                   LPT Ports: 3
                   COM Ports: 2

-------------------------- Computer ----------------------------
              Computer Name: Compaq
          BIOS Manufacturer: Compaq
               BIOS Version:
              BIOS Category: IBM PC/AT
              BIOS ID Bytes: FC 01 00
                  BIOS Date: 02/25/92
                  Processor: 80386
            Math Coprocessor: None
                   Keyboard: Enhanced
                   Bus Type: EISA
             DMA Controller: Yes
              Cascaded IRQ2: Yes
           BIOS Data Segment: 0154 -10404k

--------------------------- Memory -----------------------------
Legend: Available "  "  RAM "##"  ROM "RR"  Possibly Available ".."
EMS Page Frame "PP"  Used UMBs "UU"  Free UMBs "FF"
1024K FC00 RRRRRRRRRRRRRRRR FFFF  Conventional Memory
      F800 RRRRRRRRRRRRRRRR FBFF            Total: 639K
      F400 RRRRRRRRRRRRRRRR F7FF        Available: 352K
 960K F000 RRRRRRRRRRRRRRRR F3FF                  360480 bytes
      EC00                  EFFF
      E800                  EBFF  Extended Memory
      E400 RRRRRRRR         E7FF            Total: 11264K
 896K E000 RRRRRRRRRRRRRRRR E3FF
      DC00                  DFFF
      D800                  DBFF
      D400                  D7FF
 832K D000                  D3FF
      CC00                  CFFF
      C800                  CBFF
      C400 RRRRRRRR  . ..   C7FF
 768K C000 RRRRRRRRRRRRRRRR C3FF
      BC00 ################ BFFF
      B800 ################ BBFF
      B400                  B7FF
 704K B000                  B3FF
      AC00                  AFFF
      A800                  ABFF
      A400                  A7FF
 640K A000                  A3FF
```

```
------------------------- Video ------------------------------
            Video Adapter Type: VGA
                Manufacturer: Compaq
                       Model:
                Display Type: VGA Color
                  Video Mode: 3
           Number of Columns: 80
              Number of Rows: 25
          Video BIOS Version:
             Video BIOS Date: 08/08/91
       VESA Support Installed: No
           Secondary Adapter: None

------------------------- Network ------------------------------
            Network Detected: Yes
                Network Name: Novell
   MS-DOS Network Functions: Not Supported
             NetBIOS Present: No
               Shell Version: 3.26.00
                    Shell OS: MS-DOS
            Shell OS Version: V5.00
               Hardware Type: STDDOS
              Station Number: 5
     Physical Station Number: 0080:138F:2049
               IPX Installed: Yes
               SPX Installed: Yes
           ODI/LSL Installed: Yes

------------------------- OS Version ------------------------------
           Operating System: MS-DOS 5.00
           Internal Revision: 00
           OEM Serial Number: FFH
          User Serial Number: 000000H
          OEM Version String:
              DOS Located in: Conventional Memory
                  Boot Drive: C:
             Path to Program: W:\PUBLIC\UTILITY\MSD.EXE

              Environment Strings
              ----------------------------
ID=TJOYCE
PATH=Z:.;Y:.;X:.;W:.;V:.;U:.;
COMSPEC=Y:COMMAND.COM
MV=SONOMA\SYS:PUBLIC\
PROMPT=[MSDOS] $P$G
UID=5000028
ADDR=0080138F2049
NET=000000101%
WPC=/NT-1/U-TAJ
TEMP=F:\USERS\TJOYCE\TEMP
FULL=Teresa Anne Joyce TAJ

------------------------- Mouse ------------------------------
              Mouse Hardware: InPort Mouse
         Driver Manufacturer: No Mouse Driver

------------------------- Disk Drives ------------------------------
Drive  Type                                    Free Space  Total Size
-----  ----------------------------------      ----------  ----------
  A:   Floppy Drive, 3.5" 1.44M
       80 Cylinders, 2 Heads
       512 Bytes/Sector, 18 Sectors/Track
```

```
    B:    Floppy Drive, 5.25" 1.2M
             80 Cylinders, 2 Heads
             512 Bytes/Sector, 15 Sectors/Track
    C:    Fixed Disk, CMOS Type 50                    52M         113M
             745 Cylinders, 8 Heads
             512 Bytes/Sector, 39 Sectors/Track
          CMOS Fixed Disk Parameters
             760 Cylinders, 8 Heads
             39 Sectors/Track
    F:    Remote Drive
    G:    Remote Drive
    K:    Remote Drive
    U:    Remote Drive
    V:    Remote Drive
    W:    Remote Drive
    X:    Remote Drive
    Y:    Remote Drive
    Z:    Remote Drive
LASTDRIVE='`:
```

```
------------------------- LPT Ports ---------------------------
              Port      On     Paper    I/O    Time
    Port    Address    Line    Out     Error   Out    Busy    ACK
    -----   -------    ----    -----   -----   ----   ----    ---
    LPT1:    03BCH     No      No      No      Yes    Yes     No
    LPT2:    03BCH     No      No      No      Yes    Yes     No
    LPT3:    03BCH     No      No      No      Yes    Yes     No
```

```
------------------------- COM Ports ---------------------------
                                 COM1:    COM2:    COM3:    COM4:
                                 -----    -----    -----    -----
Port Address                     03F8H    02F8H    N/A      N/A
Baud Rate                        9600     9600
Parity                           None     None
Data Bits                        8        8
Stop Bits                        1        1
Carrier Detect (CD)              No       No
Ring Indicator (RI)              No       No
Data Set Ready (DSR)             No       No
Clear To Send (CTS)              No       No
UART Chip Used                   16550AF  16550AF
```

```
------------------------- IRQ Status ---------------------------
IRQ   Address      Description        Detected       Handled By
---   ----------   ---------------    ------------   ----------------
  0   2198:098D    Timer Click        Yes            NW.EXE
  1   2198:084E    Keyboard           Yes            NW.EXE
  2   F000:9BD0    Second 8259A       Yes            BIOS
  3   F000:9BD0    COM2: COM4:        COM2:          BIOS
  4   F000:9BD0    COM1: COM3:        COM1:          BIOS
  5   F000:9BD0    LPT2:              Yes            BIOS
  6   0E5A:00B7    Floppy Disk        Yes            Default Handlers
  7   0070:06F4    LPT1:              Yes            System Area
  8   0E5A:0052    Real-Time Clock    Yes            Default Handlers
  9   F000:9C1F    Redirected IRQ2    Yes            BIOS
 10   1202:0165    (Reserved)                        NE2000
 11   F000:9BD0    (Reserved)                        BIOS
 12   F000:9BD0    (Reserved)                        BIOS
 13   F000:9C28    Math Coprocessor   No             BIOS
 14   0E5A:0117    Fixed Disk         Yes            Default Handlers
 15   F000:9BD0    (Reserved)                        BIOS
```

```
------------------------- TSR Programs --------------------------
Program Name        Address   Size  Command Line Parameters
----------------    -------  ------  -------------------------------
System Data          0B57    14176
   File Handles      0B59      896
   FCBS              0B92      256
   BUFFERS           0BA3    10640
   Directories       0E3D      448
   Default Handlers  0E5A     1856
COMMAND.COM          0ECE     4448   tjoyce
Free Memory          0FE5       64
COMMAND.COM          0FEA      592   tjoyce
DOSKEY               1010     4128
LSL                  1113     3792   N
NE2000               1201     4000
IPXODI               12FC    15888
NETX                 16DE    43728
Free Memory          218C       80
NW.EXE               2192      224
NW.EXE               21A1     4928
LOGIN.EXE            22D6      224   tjoyce
LOGIN.EXE            22E5   139616   tjoyce
LOGIN.EXE            44FC     8192   tjoyce
TIMERUN.exe          46FD      256   /P K:\SYSTEM\REPORTS\TJOYCE.RP
TIMERUN.exe          470E     2368   /P K:\SYSTEM\REPORTS\TJOYCE.RP
TIMERUN.exe          47A3      112   /P K:\SYSTEM\REPORTS\TJOYCE.RP
MSD.EXE              47AB      272   /P K:\SYSTEM\REPORTS\TJOYCE.RP
MSD.EXE              47BD   316576   /P K:\SYSTEM\REPORTS\TJOYCE.RP
MSD.EXE              9508      640   /P K:\SYSTEM\REPORTS\TJOYCE.RP
MSD.EXE              9531    42944   /P K:\SYSTEM\REPORTS\TJOYCE.RP
TIMERUN.exe          9FAE      256   /P K:\SYSTEM\REPORTS\TJOYCE.RP
Free Memory          9FBF        0

----------------------- Device Drivers ------------------------
   Device        Filename  Units    Header        Attributes
   ------------  --------  -----   ---------    ----------------
   NUL                             0116:0048    1...........1..
   CON                             0070:0023    1.........1..11
   AUX                             0070:0035    1..............
   PRN                             16DF:6616    1...1..........
   CLOCK$                          0070:0059    1............1...
   Block Device            3       0070:006B    ....1...11....1.
   COM1                            0070:007B    1..............
   LPT1                            16DF:6628    1...1..........
   LPT2                            16DF:663A    1...1..........
   LPT3                            16DF:664C    1...1..........
   COM2                            0070:00CA    1..............
   COM3                            0070:00DC    1..............
   COM4                            0070:00EE    1..............
----------------------- C:\AUTOEXEC.BAT ----------------------
   @ECHO OFF
   PROMPT=$P$G
   DOSKEY
   LSL
   NE2000
   IPXODI
   NETX
   PREFER SONOMA
   NETDRIVE
   LOGIN.
```

```
----------------------- C:\CONFIG.SYS --------------------------
    SHELL=C:\COMMAND.COM /E:512 /P
    BUFFERS=20
    FILES=20
.
.
LOGIN NAME:   TJOYCE
.
 FULL NAME:   Teresa Anne Joyce TAJ
.
   USER ID:   5000028
.
   NETWORK:   00000101%
.
#rem   ACCOUNT_EXPIRATION     <no restrictions>
#rem   PASSWORD_PERIOD        <no restrictions>
#rem   PASSWORD_REQUIRED      <no restrictions>
#rem   UNIQUE_PASSWORD        <no restrictions>
#rem   CONNECTIONS            <no restrictions>
#rem   TIME RESTRICTIONS      <no restrictions>
#rem   MAX_DISK_SPACE         <no restrictions>
#groups STAFF;
#rem   STATIONS               <no restrictions>
#rem   Trustee Assignments:
#rem      [ RWCEMF ]    SYS:PUBLIC/MHS/MAIL/USERS/TJOYCE/NW
#rem      [ RWCEMF ]    SYS:PUBLIC/MHS/MAIL/USERS/TJOYCE/IPARCEL
#rem      [ RWCEMF ]    SYS:PUBLIC/MHS/MAIL/USERS/TJOYCE/FIRST
#rem      [ RWCEMF ]    SYS:PUBLIC/MHS/MAIL/USERS/TJOYCE
#rem      [ RWCEMFA]    SYS:USERS/TJOYCE
#create TJOYCE;Teresa Anne Joyce TAJ;TJOYCE;^
##RESET
.
.
MS-DOS Version 5.00
Revision A
DOS is in low memory
.
    ==END OF REPORT==
```

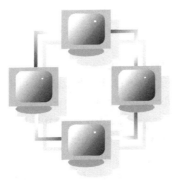

4

Building Reliable Systems

*B*efore you take any steps toward disaster recovery, you need to focus on those things that make your system reliable. LAN reliability is not something you add on; it is created by a combination of hardware, software, design, planning and installation. This chapter will focus on the factors that affect system reliability and the things you can do to increase the reliability of your LAN.

Planning, Design and Installation

Most continuously recurring network problems can be attributed to poor planning, design or installation. Unfortunately, many networks were never planned or designed, they "just happened." Installation is often just as haphazard, with LAN components being installed by people with little experience with or understanding of networks. As LANs grow and expand, the effects of things such as improperly installed or incorrect cable and poorly designed server directory structures are amplified, turning seemingly minor problems into major ones. Cleaning up design and installation problems is the first step toward building a reliable system.

Cabling System

The cabling system is probably the most critical set of components of your network. A poorly designed or installed cabling system can be difficult to troubleshoot and can cause many needless hours of downtime.

Maintainable Design. A good cabling system is designed for reliability, manageability and maintainability. Older linear cabling systems, such as the original Ethernet and Thin Ethernet systems, were not designed with troubleshooting in mind. However, modern star-wired systems, including those used for 10BASE-T Ethernet and Token Ring, are much easier to manage and maintain.

One of the best cabling design guides is *Commercial Building Wiring Standard: ANSI/EIA/TIA-568-4966*, available from the Electronic Industry Association at 202/457-4966. This document is the result of a coordinated effort by several industry standards groups to create a standard approach to data cabling.

Proper Installation. Finding a knowledgeable installer for LAN cabling is not always easy. Many companies and individuals who are experienced with telephone cabling, for example, assume that they understand LAN cabling. Although both can use the same types of wire, the design considerations are very different. A basic difference is that telephones generate low-frequency signals (under 1 Mhz[1]) while LANs generate high-frequency signals (1 Mhz to 100 Mhz or more). Installation practices that work for telephone systems may not work for LANs. Make sure your installer understands LAN cabling and that ANSI/EIA/TIA-568 guidelines are followed.

See that proper cable types and grades are used and all cable lengths kept within specifications. In addition, make sure that proper connectors and connection blocks are used. This is especially critical when you are attempting to build cabling systems that follow ANSI/EIA/TIA Category 4 or 5 specifications. (See *Cabling System and Components* below.)

Document your cabling system. A good cabling diagram and properly labeled cables and wall plates will help eliminate wasted time when you are troubleshooting cabling problems. (See Chapter 3.)

Wiring Closets and Hubs. Hubs (aka concentrators, multistation access units and MAUs) and wiring closets are the nerve centers of your network. Here are a few tips to help you manage them:

■ Make sure the wiring closet has proper ventilation, heating and cooling, even on weekends and holidays. Network hubs and other equipment can fail if temperatures are too high or too low.

■ If the wiring closet is shared with telephone equipment or more than one type of LAN is sharing a closet, use separate connector panels or color-coded connector blocks for each system. This will help prevent crossed connections that can bring down a network.

---

[1]Megahertz, or millions of cycles per second.

- Clearly mark all panels and connectors so that mistakes do not happen.

- Make sure that proper power protection is provided to hubs and other components. If critical connections must be maintained during a power outage, make sure that the hubs used for those connections are attached to appropriate power backup systems.

- Make sure those who have access to the closet know the "rules of the road." This means making sure that everyone, including outside contractors, understands the layout of the closet, what connects to what, and how to make connections in a consistent manner.

- Keep patch cable length to a minimum. Patch cables that are too long get in the way when you are trying to track down cabling problems.

- Make sure that you and your support staff have immediate access to wiring closets. In some office buildings, building management keeps wiring closets locked and requires you to obtain special permission to enter, as well as find someone with the keys. This makes emergency troubleshooting and repair difficult at best and nearly impossible on evenings and weekends. If you have a similar situation, you need to find some way to gain access on an as-needed basis.

- Only those who have a legitimate need should have access to wiring closets. Wiring closets are potentially a major source of security compromise.

Servers and Hosts

Servers and hosts include file servers, database servers, communications servers, mail servers, host gateways, application servers and time-sharing hosts. Make sure that these systems are installed in areas with proper ventilation, heating and cooling, even on weekends and holidays. Proper power protection is also important. For security reasons physical access should be controlled, especially for file servers and time-sharing hosts.

Where possible, maintain consistency of systems and components. Problem resolution is easier with fewer types and brands of CPUs, LAN cards, disk systems and so on. This approach also makes it easier and less costly to maintain spares.

Workstations and Components

As with servers, maintaining consistency makes troubleshooting easier and reduces the cost of maintaining spares. Consistency also provides for interchangeability of workstations, making it easier to swap out a defective system in an emergency.

System Software and Logical Structures

Setting up system software in a consistent manner will make troubleshooting and problem resolution easier. This means standardizing file server directory structures, user names, boot files, login scripts and menus. Consistency and standardization in these areas makes troubleshooting easier because you don't have to learn a new approach with every system, user or application.

Setting up directories on a network file server is a little different from setting up directories on a stand-alone PC. Logical organization for use by a single user is usually the primary concern on a stand-alone PC. On a file server, however, you must be concerned with logical organization for use by multiple users, as well as security and access control (see Figure 4-1).

A file server directory should take the best advantage possible of the network operating system's security. In addition, it should be readable by you and others so that it can be easily maintained.

User accounts should be as consistent as possible. By using, for example, a standard naming scheme for user names and home directories, you ease the job of maintenance.

Figure 4-1: Sample File Server Directory Structure

```
(file_server)/SYS:╤═►SYSTEM══════╤═►040015
                  ║              └─►1A00AD
                  ╠═►LOGIN
                  ╠═►MAIL════════╤═►1
                  ║              ├─►2010B
                  ║              └─►50023
                  ╠═►PUBLIC══════╤═►IBM_PC═══════►MSDOS═╤═►V3.30
                  ║              ║                      └─►V5.00
                  ║              ├─►COMPAQ══════►MSDOS══►V5.00
                  ║              ├─►NOVELL══════►MSDOS══►V3.31
                  ║              ├─►TANDY═══════►MSDOS══►V3.30
                  ║              ├─►BATCH
                  ║              └─►UTILITY
                  ╠═►DOSAPPS═════╤═►LOTUS
                  ║              ├─►WINDOWS
                  ║              └─►WP51═══════════╤═►SETUP
                  ║                                └─►FONTS
                  ╠═►GROUPS══════╤═►ACCTING
                  ║              └─►SALES
                  ╠═►MACAPPS═════╤═►EXCEL
                  ║              ├─►PAGEMAKE
                  ║              └─►WORDPERF
                  ╠═►USERS═══════╤═►KCONKLIN
                  ║              ├─►PCORRIGA
                  ║              └─►TJOYCE
                  └─►WINAPPS═════╤═►GAMES
                                 ├─►LZFN
                                 └─►LZFW
```

Application Software

When installing applications, follow the directory structure guidelines outlined above. Unfortunately, many application developers assume that their product is the most important (or only) application you will use; therefore, they assume that it is no problem to force you to use their directory structure, and it is no problem if they modify your AUTOEXEC.BAT files, CONFIG.SYS files, login scripts and so on without warning. If you are going to keep your systems manageable, you need to maintain control over how applications are installed instead of letting the applications' install defaults exercise the control. This isn't always easy, but the following tips may help:

- Keep it simple. When installing applications, avoid complex batch files and convoluted directory structures.

- Create user-specific or user-modifiable configuration files in each user's home directory so that there are no conflicts when multiple users access the same application. An exception might be a program such as WordPerfect,™ which allows you to put configuration files in one or more shared directories and globally update them.

- Use environment variables for "environment-specific" configuration files. Several public-domain and shareware utilities are available that set DOS environment variables for video type, keyboard type and so on. Effective use of these utilities can help you make sure that users find the correct versions of applications or configuration files for their hardware.

- Before installing any application, perform a full backup of your file server and workstation. Copy any AUTOEXEC.BAT, CONFIG.SYS and login script files to other file names (but don't use the extensions .BAK, .TMP or .SAV). Find out *EXACTLY* what the installation utilities do. If a batch file is used for installation, print it out. If there is an install program, read the documentation. If the documentation is not explicit, call the vendor to obtain the information. Make sure the install program is not going to damage any of your existing files.

- Avoid installing an application in a volume's root directory! With most network operating systems, if you grant users rights to the root directory, you have to explicitly exclude them from subdirectories.

■   After installing an application, make sure you set the proper file attributes to allow the application to be shared (or not shared), if necessary.

■   Make sure you create or modify any login scripts, menus, batch files and so on to give users access to the applications and files.

■   Make sure you grant the appropriate access rights to the application directories.

■   Log in with a standard user account to test the application. As Supervisor you have all rights; therefore, you will not be able to tell how the application will work for users.

Application Installation and Testing. Applications that are not properly installed and tested can cause data loss and downtime. Applications should be tested for:

■   LAN compatibility

■   Multiple-user access (file locking, file attributes), if applicable

■   Multi-user functionality (record locking, file locking, file attributes), if applicable

■   User access (i.e., proper directory and file rights)

■   Compatibility with multiple workstation environments, including DOS (or other operating system) versions, video types, processor types and RAM requirements

■   Multi-platform file compatibility (DOS, UNIX,™ Macintosh)

■   Test applications after seemingly unrelated changes. Application testing rules of thumb:

- Perform initial tests on special test systems or when all or most users are not logged in.

- Test with user accounts that have rights levels similar to those of actual users.

- "Roll out" new applications to a few test users before putting them in general use. Make sure that your test users have an effective method of reporting and resolving problems.

Hardware and Software Selection

Choosing network components is not always easy. The good news is that, in most cases, you have a lot of choices. That, unfortunately, is also the bad news, because someone has to make those choices. You will have to weigh the factors of performance, cost, compatibility, reliability and adherence to standards. You must balance the components of the system to achieve optimum performance and reliability at reasonable cost.

An additional problem is that the LAN administrator or IS manager does not always make the decision on which components to purchase. Purchase decisions are often based on such factors as user preference, company policy, decisions made by a purchasing department or specific, specialized needs. In other words, in most organizations you will not be able to comprehensively test each and every component before it is installed on your LAN. You will need to deal with problems caused by some of those components.

So how do you assure that components being added to your system are appropriate and reliable?

Some organizations establish company standards that dictate what components users can and cannot buy. There are several problems with this approach:

- There will always be special cases that the standards don't cover. This means that exceptions will have to be granted.

- Users will ignore the standards if they need something non-standard (and they think they can get away with it). This means that "standards police" will have to enforce the standards. It also means that problems caused by non-standard components may be difficult to trace since the existence of those components will not be reported.

- Without a concerted effort to constantly test and review new products, corporate standards will quickly get out of date.

- The procedure for establishing company standards in most organizations is usually slow, cumbersome and fraught with politics. Turf battles are common in the realm of standards.

Other organizations provide guidelines, but not necessarily strict standards. These organizations will usually provide support and/or training for approved products but not necessarily for unapproved ones. Instead of forbidding unapproved products, they make it attractive for users to select approved ones.

In most organizations there are certain products that are proscribed, usually due to past negative experiences or known incompatibilities with existing products.

As LANs grow larger and more complex, it becomes increasingly difficult to set or enforce standards or guidelines. At some point, someone will add something to your LAN that will affect its operation, approved or not.

© Joe Troise and Phil Frank

Your best defenses against problems of this sort are education and user cooperation. LAN administrators need to have up-to-the-minute knowledge of and information about potential problems. Monitoring the support forums on CompuServe, the Internet and vendors' support BBSes is a good start here. By monitoring the problems others are having with particular products, you can avoid or correct those problems in your system.

User cooperation is important when troubleshooting. If users feel like they're "helping the enemy" by giving you information (an attitude often held by users when the IS or tech support people approach things in a dictatorial fashion), your troubleshooting job will be much more difficult than it should be.

Guidelines for Product Selection

■ **Follow industry standards when and where they apply.** Adherence to industry standards usually means that products from many vendors will work together. It often means lower cost because standardization creates competition, lowering prices.

Standards can be *de jure*, meaning sanctioned by some recognized standards body, or *de facto*, meaning standard by virtue of acceptance. An example of a *de jure* standard is the IEEE 802.3 standard for Ethernet-type networks. An example of a *de facto* standard is the expansion bus used in the IBM PC-AT and hundreds of clones. The AT bus, now referred to as the *industry standard architecture (ISA)* bus, became a standard because buyers of computers (after some initial help from IBM) have made it the most used computer expansion bus in history.

Just because something is declared a standard by a standards body or the press doesn't mean that it will benefit you or that it is even a standard. Standards are not created by the pronouncement of one vendor. They are created by acceptance in the marketplace.

- **Balance the need for standardization with the needs for functionality and cost effectiveness.** Don't follow standards that don't help you. Just because a product meets some standard does not mean that it is the best for your purposes, the most cost-effective or the most widely accepted.

  For example, *Fiber Distributed Data Interface (FDDI)* is an *American National Standards Institute (ANSI)* standard for 100 Mbps token-passing networks. Although it is an official standard, and FDDI products are manufactured by several companies, proprietary TCNS™ from Thomas-Conrad Corporation outsells it, according to one study, by a factor of two to one. One reason for this is that TCNS interface cards are considerably less expensive than equivalent FDDI cards. They are also easier to acquire through standard distribution channels. Several benchmarks have also shown TCNS out-performing FDDI. The downside, however, is that TCNS is only produced by one manufacturer, and if you decide that you do not like their products or policies, or they go out of business (not likely, but it has happened in the computer industry), you are somewhat stuck.

- **Use easily available, off-the-shelf components.** After Hurricane Andrew destroyed the Miami headquarters of database software vendor Data Access Corporation, the company was back up and running in a new location in a matter of days. One of the reasons for this, according to Data Access President Charles Casanave, was that "we made a conscious decision to build our LAN using easily available, standard PCs and components."

  Unfortunately, many vendors will try to lock you into their products by supplying proprietary components, often justified for performance reasons. For example, some disk system vendors supply software drivers (or even ROM code on host adapters) that require you to buy specially "signatured" disks from them at (usually) inflated prices. The major problem with this approach, however, is not the extra cost of the drives but the fact that you are limited to a single source of supply. This can be a severe problem in event of a disaster if that company cannot supply a replacement quickly or has gone out of business.

Cabling System and Components

The type of cabling system you select will affect the ease with which you will be able to locate and resolve many LAN problems. Here are some general guidelines for selecting a cabling system and topology:

■ Use a star topology. A star topology, as used by Token Ring and 10BASE-T Ethernet, is much easier to troubleshoot than a linear system, such as 10BASE-2 or 10BASE-5 Ethernet.

■ Consider using unshielded twisted-pair wire (UTP). The advantage of UTP over other cable types is that it is almost universal in application. Nearly all major LAN architectures currently run on UTP, giving you a great deal of flexibility.

There are different grades of UTP, and not all of it is suitable for all LANs. Underwriter's Laboratories (UL) has specified five performance levels for UTP, designated Level I through Level V. Levels III, IV and V are specified for networks operating above 1 Mbps, with Level V being the highest performance level, designed to transmit data at higher speeds over longer distances than the lower levels. UL levels III through V correspond to the Electronic Industry Association/Telecommunications Industry Association (EIA/TIA) Categories 3 through 5. It is important to note that these levels and categories apply to all cabling components, including connectors and punch-down blocks. In other words, in a Category 5 system, all components must correspond to Category 5 specifications.

Category 5 is not required for most current LAN installations. If you are installing new cabling, however, installing Category 5 cabling will probably benefit you when you eventually upgrade to a faster LAN.

■ Plan for fiber optics. Fiber is expensive now, but costs will go down as usage increases. Proper planning now will make it easier to install fiber later.

■ Use intelligent hubs with SNMP management. Intelligent hubs can be monitored and controlled from a PC or terminal. Most hub vendors supply management software for their own intelligent hubs. Often, however, that software is proprietary to that vendor's product. Simple Network Management Protocol (SNMP), part of the TCP/IP protocol suite, is fast becoming the standard LAN management and monitoring protocol. Although significant roadblocks still exist, SNMP is on its way to true interoperability, where any SNMP manager can manage any SNMP-compliant device. Although SNMP originally required TCP/IP, a number of SNMP managers can now use other protocols, such as Novell's IPX.

■ Keep spares for patch cables, hubs (or hub cards) and other components.

EIA/TIA, in conjunction with ANSI, has published a set of guidelines for office cabling called *Commercial Building Wiring Standard: ANSI/EIA/TIA-568-4966*. This document is available from the Electronic Industry Association at 202/457-4966.

File Servers

File servers fall into three main categories: proprietary, generic and specialized. Proprietary servers, common in the mid-to-late 1980s, have virtually disappeared. Proprietary servers usually worked only with one vendor's LAN hardware and software. When a proprietary server's useful life as a file server was over, there was little you could do with it other than perhaps turn it into a planter. Proprietary servers were useful, from the vendor's point of view, because they tended to lock you into that vendor's products. To be fair, they sometimes had features that enhanced the operation of the vendor's LAN OS.

Generic servers are general-purpose computers used as file servers. Standard Intel processor-based PCs are probably the most common type of generic file server and the most widely used file server platform. Advantages of generic servers include low cost, ease of repair or replacement, and reusability. Once they are no longer useful as file servers, they can be used as workstations, print servers or for other purposes.

Generic servers can be "name-brand" PCs or "clones," although the distinction is beginning to blur. Here is one definition: name-brand PCs are those that have national advertising and distribution, while clones are built in smaller shops and sold locally or regionally. This definition does not address issues such as quality, reliability or compatibility with industry standards because name-brand products do not seem to be any better or worse in these areas than clones. The real issue here is supportability. The major advantage of name-brand PCs over clones (as file servers) is that you stand a somewhat better chance of finding someone who can help you with machine-specific problems when you use name-brand PCs. In addition to manufacturer technical support departments (which, by the way, many clone vendors have), information concerning problems with name-brand systems is often available from dealers, user groups and on-line information forums.

Specialized servers are designed or sold specifically as file servers. They usually have features or attributes that, according to the vendor, make them uniquely suited to file service. Those features may include proprietary, high-performance LAN or disk adapters, redundant power supplies, extra expansion slots, room for more than the usual number of disk drives, multiple processors or even dual, redundant servers in a single box. In most cases, specialized servers use the same CPUs as generic servers.

When deciding between generic and specialized servers, consider the following:

■   You can often buy two generic servers (especially if you use external disk subsystems) for the cost of one specialized server.

■   Specialized servers often use proprietary components, and these may be difficult to obtain quickly in case of emergency. Upgrades can also be more costly than with generic servers.

■   Specialized servers do not always lend themselves to being used as workstations after their useful server life is over.

Multiple File Servers. When should you use multiple file servers, and when should you consolidate servers? Multiple file servers are usually used for three purposes: performance, security and manageability.

If a server's CPU is running out of steam, it may be time to add another server. It may also be time, however, to investigate the reasons for poor performance. Poor performance can be caused by numerous things, including LAN and disk I/O bottlenecks, limited file server RAM, improperly set server parameters, or poorly written applications. Upgrading or replacing a slow server to alleviate performance problems may be a better solution than adding another server. Each time you add a file server, you increase your management overhead.

Security and manageability are the two major reasons for adding file servers. In many organizations, servers are managed on the department level, and it makes sense in those situations to have separate departmental servers. Also, some departments or workgroups have data on their servers that is extremely sensitive; these groups may also want to manage their own servers.

Disk Drives for Servers

Over the last few years disk drives have become more reliable. Still, they do occasionally fail, and you need to be prepared for that eventuality. You have numerous choices of interfaces, drive capacities and fault-tolerant configurations.

Which Interface? Almost all current-model hard disks use one of two interfaces, *Intelligent Drive Electronics* (IDE) or *Small Computer Systems Interface* (SCSI). Earlier interfaces that were popular in the PC arena, including MFM, RLL and ESDI, have pretty much faded away.

IDE. IDE seems to be the drive interface of choice for Intel processor-based desktop PCs. IDE drives and adapters are generally very cost-effective, but capacities are usually 500 MB or less. An IDE adapter (often called a "paddle board" because it contains so few components) can support two drives. Unlike the earlier MFM, RLL and ESDI drives, where the *controller* electronics resided on the adapter board that plugged into the PC, the controller electronics reside on the IDE drive itself. Depending on the operating system, one or two paddle boards can be installed in a PC. The first drive is the *master*, the second the *slave*. If the first drive fails, the second drive is unavailable. If the second drive fails, the first drive spends a lot of time looking for it, and some operating systems can time-out and not load. IDE drives are fine for small-capacity file servers where disk redundancy is not required, but expansion capabilities are limited.

SCSI. SCSI drives are common in the Macintosh arena and also commonly used in network file servers. There are several varieties of SCSI, and they are all slightly different, but they share certain attributes. Like IDE drives, the controller electronics are generally built into SCSI drives. While an IDE adapter can only support two drives, an SCSI adapter can support up to seven devices, including hard disks, read/write optical disks, CD-ROMs and tape drives. Depending on the operating system, up to four or five SCSI adapters can be attached to one PC. In addition, devices connected to an SCSI adapter operate independently, with none being a master or slave. In general, SCSI provides better performance, flexibility and expandability than IDE.

RAID and Drive Redundancy. Redundant disk drives allow non-stop operation in case of a drive failure. The acronym RAID stands for *Redundant Array of Inexpensive Disks.* Six levels of RAID, 0 through 5, were defined in a paper published by the University of California at Berkeley in 1988 by David Patterson, Garth Gibson and Randy Katz titled *A Case for Redundant Array of Inexpensive Disks (RAID).*

RAID 0—Data Striping with Block Interleaving. With RAID 0, data is written across all drives. Data is written to disk a block at a time, with each block written sequentially to the next drive (called *block interleaving*). Block size is determined by the operating system, but usually ranges from 2 KB to 64 KB. Depending on the design of the disk controllers, these sequential writes can overlap, and overlapping writes can increase performance. If a drive fails, the complete subsystem fails, generally with a complete loss of data. Used by itself, RAID 0 can provide performance improvements and larger single-volume size, but does not provide fault tolerance.

A variation of data striping is *drive spanning and data scattering*. With drive spanning, data is written across multiple disks sequentially. Unlike data striping, however, writes do not have to be made to every disk. If a disk is busy (or full), data can be written to the next available disk. This allows disks to be added to an existing volume. Like RAID 0, drive spanning used by itself can provide performance improvements and larger single-volume size, but does not provide fault tolerance.

RAID 1—Disk Mirroring or Duplexing. With disk mirroring, the same data is written to two disks. If one disk fails, the system can continue to operate off the paired disk. Novell, Inc. has narrowed the definition of mirroring and has added the term *duplexing*. Using Novell terminology, mirroring refers to drives connected to a file server or host computer using a single host bus adapter. Duplexing refers to drives (or groups of drives) attached with separate host bus adapters. Duplexing provides for redundance of the entire *disk channel*, including host bus adapters, cables and drives.

RAID 2—Data Striping with Bit Interleaving. Data is written across all drives one bit at a time (called *bit interleaving*). Checksum information is written to separate drives, called *checksum drives*. This is extremely slow because every drive in the array must be accessed for every write. RAID 2 also requires multiple checksum drives, which increases the cost and complexity. RAID 2 is rarely, if ever, used in small systems.

RAID 3—Data Striping with Bit Interleaving and Parity Checking. Like RAID 2, data is written across all drives one bit at a time. Instead of checksum information, for each byte written a parity bit is written to a single *parity* drive. Like RAID 2, every drive must be accessed for every write. RAID 3 is somewhat more reliable than RAID 2, because the chance of one parity drive failing is lower than the chance of one of three checksum drives failing.

RAID 4—Data Striping with Block Interleaving and Parity Checking. RAID 4 combines the block data striping of RAID 0 with the parity checking and single parity drive of RAID 3. Like RAID 2 and 3, every drive must be accessed for every write.

RAID 5—Data Striping with Block Interleaving and Distributed Parity. RAID 5 provides block data striping across all drives without the need for a dedicated parity drive. The data and checksum are striped at the sector level across the entire array. This technique allows independent reads and writes and allows multiple concurrent I/O operations. A drive only needs to be accessed if data or parity information is being written to or read from it. Because of the multiple I/O capability, and because all drives are not involved in each write, performance can be considerably higher than that of RAID 2, 3 and 4.

Novell's Mirroring, Duplexing and Drive Spanning. Novell's disk mirroring and duplexing implement RAID 1. In addition, NetWare allows you to combine RAID 1 with drive spanning and data scattering (similar to RAID 0). When spanned drives are duplexed (separate host bus adapters for each channel), NetWare allows split seeks on read operations, meaning that data can be read from alternate channels in high-traffic situations. Because NetWare uses data scattering instead of data striping, drives can be added to existing volumes.

By default, NetWare implements HotFix, which provides for on-the-fly bad block repair during write operations. Using read-after-write verification, NetWare detects errors and redirects data being written to a bad block to another area of the disk.

Fault Tolerance. With the exception of RAID 0 and 1, the fault tolerance of the various RAID levels is almost identical, that is, each array technique from RAID 2 through RAID 5 can continue to function with the loss of a single drive. If a second drive fails, the entire array will fail. For this reason, it is important to perform proper backups and to immediately repair any failure that occurs in the array subsystem. Most RAID 3 through 5 systems support *hot-swapping*, or the ability to remove and replace a failed drive without disabling the array. Some systems also support *hot-spares*, which are spare drives in the array that can automatically replace a drive if it should fail.

RAID 0 provides no fault tolerance, while RAID 1, mirroring, can tolerate the loss of a single mirrored drive or, if multiple drives are mirrored, any or all drives in one half of a mirrored pair. NetWare's drive spanning and data scattering, like RAID 0, provides no fault tolerance (other than HotFix) unless it is used in conjunction with mirroring or duplexing.

Performance. Depending on the operating system being used, some RAID implementations can provide increased performance. However, with an operating system that is already highly optimized for disk access, such as Novell's NetWare, performance may actually be degraded. In addition, RAID 3 through 5 systems require more processing than standard disk drives. Most RAID 3 systems use intelligent array controllers to take the processing load off of the host computer's CPU, while some RAID 5 systems use multiple host adapters to increase performance.

Expandability. Because RAID 3 through 5 systems use data striping, drives must be identical in size, and you cannot add a drive without reinitializing the entire array. With mirroring or duplexing with data scattering, you can easily add drives in pairs.

Proprietary or Non-Proprietary Design. Some RAID 3 through 5 systems require specially *signatured* drives that are only available from the array manufacturer, often at inflated prices. In addition, many array systems use other proprietary components, such as array controllers, that are also only available from the manufacturer. Aside from increased cost, one problem with this is that those drives or components are only available from that vendor, and if that vendor goes out of business or is temporarily out of inventory, you have no second source. This can be a major problem in an emergency.

Single Points of Failure. Some RAID systems have possible single points of failure that you need to watch for. For example, one system has three power supplies, but a single power cord, switch and fuse!

Cost. Because RAID 3 through 5 use fewer drives, for equivalent disk capacity, than mirrored or duplexed systems, conventional wisdom would suggest that RAID 3 through 5 systems would cost less than mirrored or duplexed systems. Multiple host bus adapters, intelligent array controllers and proprietary components, however, can mean that RAID 3 and 5 systems can cost as much as or more than duplexed and mirrored systems. RAID prices are falling rapidly, however, as competition increases.

Internal versus External Drive Systems. External drive systems have a major advantage over internal systems—a drive system can be removed and replaced without disassembling the file server. If you are employing Novell's duplexing with separate SCSI adapters and separate external subsystems for each disk channel, you can power down a subsystem with a failed disk, disconnect it, repair it and reinstall it without bringing down your file server. The downside to external systems is increased cost.

One other advantage of external systems is low-cost server redundancy. If you maintain a backup file server, properly configured with disk host adapters and sufficient RAM, you can quickly and easily replace a defective server in a few minutes by powering it down, unplugging its disk systems and then plugging them into your backup server. In most cases, this will result in little lost data or time.

Client Workstations

One advantage of LAN technology is support for a diverse range of desktop computers. Unfortunately, for a LAN administrator that diversity can be a support nightmare! Here are some tips to help make the job easier.

■   When possible, standardize within each class of machines. This means fewer vendors to deal with when problems occur. Since the product life (not useful life, but how long the product will be on the market) of the average PC model in 1993 was about 15 months (and getting shorter), it is virtually impossible to standardize on particular models. In addition, the fact that more powerful processors are becoming available at a rapid rate (as well as newer applications which want to use that extra power) makes standardizing on particular models even less desirable.

The key issues here are support and interchangeability of components. As much as you try to standardize, however, users will find reasons (and often good ones) to buy equipment that is not on your standard list. One way to handle this is to broaden your list of supported products as much as is feasible. Also, work with users when they are selecting equipment. By listening to their needs, you might be able to either find equivalent products from your standard list, or you may find that you need to make changes in that list to accommodate those needs.

■   Store data and programs on file servers and use workstation hard disks for configuration files. This provides three benefits: regular workstation hard disk backup is no longer critical; if you experience a site disaster that requires you to move your operation to a temporary facility with new machines, you do not have to worry about the time it will take to load local data; and because you don't have to restore user programs and data from backup, you can replace a user's workstation quickly and have her or him up and running in a matter of minutes rather than days.

Due to either a fear of loss of control or bad experiences in the past with botched LAN installations, some users will be reluctant to store their data on file servers. If your systems are not reliable, or if you have lax security policies that don't adequately protect their data, they have good reason for their reluctance! If your systems are reliable and your security adequate, however, it should not be difficult to convince users of the benefits of central storage, including regular backup, and greater security than they have locally. (With most PCs, anyone who has access to the PC, even the janitor, has access to its data!)

■ Standardize on configurations, such as directory structures, batch files, configuration files and memory managers. This not only helps you when you are troubleshooting problems; it also makes it easier to swap machines in an emergency.

Bridges, Routers, Communications Servers and Other Components

There are numerous LAN system components that can cause downtime if they fail or are otherwise unavailable. This includes bridges, routers, communications servers, modems, CSU/DSUs, host gateways, e-mail servers and fax servers.

From a disaster planning point of view, the major factors to look at here are availability in case of emergency and ease of repair or replacement. You want to make sure that you can obtain replacements or spares quickly, and repair or install them with a minimum of time and effort. Unfortunately, not all vendors can provide this. For example, some router vendors are quoting six months or more to deliver a new router. Software-based routers, such as the

LAN^{2}LAN™ from Newport Systems Solutions and the MPR™ from Novell, Inc., use off-the-shelf components that are easily available and relatively low in cost. These types of products, although not as sophisticated as most dedicated routers, offer short learning curves, multiprotocol support and impressive performance for their cost.

Communications Links

If a backhoe at a construction site cut through one of your major communications links, how much of an effect would it have on your business? Can you afford that line to be down for an hour, a day or a week? If not, you need to consider alternate communications links using different physical paths. Be careful here, even if you use two different carriers. Carriers often share each other's lines, so you could end up with all communications using the same path anyway. If this is critical, hire someone who knows the communications systems in your area to make sure you are actually getting different data paths.

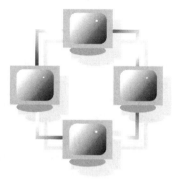

## 5

LAN Security

*S*ecurity is often viewed as being important only in large companies or government agencies. However, security is important in all organizations. LAN security is not implemented just to keep the "bad guys" from doing dastardly deeds; it is also used to keep the rest of us from causing inadvertent or accidental damage.

Implementing security appropriately requires a balance between protecting resources and allowing users the freedom needed to do their jobs well.

LAN security should not be used as a substitute for user education or just to make things more convenient for LAN administrators. For example, some LAN administrators try to keep users working within very narrow limits, making sure that they can only access those resources that they have a clearly defined need to use, or not allowing a user to exit from a menu or user interface to an operating system prompt. In other words, they remove a user's ability to use the system in a flexible manner, and flexibility is one of the main reasons for using personal computers in the first place.

"THIS SECURITY PROGRAM WILL RESPOND TO THREE THINGS: AN INCORRECT ACCESS CODE, AN INAPPROPRIATE FILE REQUEST, OR SOMETIMES A CRAZY HUNCH THAT MAYBE YOU'RE JUST ANOTHER SLIME-BALL WITH MISAPPROPRIATION OF SECURED DATA ON HIS MIND."

Although security and access control are necessary, going overboard usually engenders resentment and hostility, and actually makes the administrator's job more difficult, not easier. The key, however, is implementing sufficient levels of security in a manner that has the least impact on users' ability to get their jobs done.

Why Is LAN Security Important?

As LANs and personal computers have matured, more and more *mission-critical* applications and data have migrated from mainframes and minicomputers to PC-based LAN servers. Without proper security, these applications and data are susceptible to accidental damage or deletion, unauthorized access or sabotage. In addition, in larger organizations, the LAN is becoming the primary connection to corporate mainframes and minicomputers.

Corporate data is a valuable asset, and its loss or theft can be costly. The wrong data in the hands of a competitor can devastate a company. Laws can also mandate that some data, such as certain types of personnel data, be kept confidential. Allowing access to this type of data can be damaging to individuals and open a company to legal liability.

LAN Security Rules of Thumb

There are several very simple rules that can make the job of maintaining LAN security easier:

- **User education is key.** The best security measures in the world can have little effect if computer system users do not understand them and follow them. Users need to know why security is important, what needs to be protected and their roles in maintaining that security.

One important note here: scare tactics usually don't work, especially in the long term. Another approach that doesn't work is *security by ignorance*—assuming that if you keep access information secret no one will figure it out. This often takes the form of assuming that users are too stupid to figure something out, like modifying a CONFIG.SYS file or getting around a login script. Whenever you assume that others are less knowledgeable or less capable than yourself, you can set yourself up for unpleasant surprises.

■ **Passive security measures work better than active ones.** Whenever security measures are too complex, people will bypass them. There is a famous story about teenagers with a scanner intercepting a sensitive call from a high Reagan administration official in Air Force One (the Presidential plane) to the White House because the official was not willing to spend the time necessary to enter the proper codes to secure the call. If the security system was designed to secure the call automatically, this never would have happened.

■ **Not all data is sensitive, and some data is less sensitive than other data.** Use reasonable precautions and security guidelines. Using the same high levels of security for all data and resources makes users doubt the need for security and ignore security measures.

■ **Most data becomes less sensitive with the passage of time.** Periodically review your security requirements and adjust them when appropriate.

■ **Login scripts and startup files are not part of security.** Login scripts and batch files can easily be defeated or bypassed.

■ **Physical security of servers and other critical devices is important.** Any computer system is vulnerable if it is physically accessible.

■ **Security should be designed to protect against accidental damage, not just unauthorized access.** Accidental damage or data loss is more common than sabotage or theft of data.

■ **With the advent of low-cost, software-based protocol analyzers, data encryption across the network cable is becoming increasingly important.** Protocol analyzers can be used to view the contents of data packets and, in the hands of a knowledgeable user, to access unauthorized data. Protocol analyzers used to be available only as dedicated devices that cost many thousands of dollars, but now they are also available as software that costs as little as a few hundred dollars or less. In fact, there is at least one Ethernet protocol analyzer available at no cost from bulletin boards and on-line information services. This means that any PC can be a protocol analyzer. Until LANs move away from the current shared cable approach to switched connections, the potential exists for protocol analyzers to be used for unauthorized data access.

Physical Access Control

The first step in LAN security is controlling physical access to critical or sensitive hardware.

File Servers and Hosts

Network file servers and time-sharing hosts are especially vulnerable. If the wrong person has physical access and sufficient time and knowledge, that person will be able to access the data on that computer. Physical access control also lessens the threat of theft.

Wiring Closets and Hubs

A few years ago, a consultant in San Francisco received a call from a panicked client saying that part of their LAN was down. When the consultant walked into the wiring closet, he discovered that power cord to one of his client's ARCNET hubs had been unplugged and a piece of new telephone equipment plugged in instead. With some coordination and access control, this could have been avoided. The wiring closet is the nerve center of the LAN and needs to be protected.

Bridges, Routers, Gateways, Communication Servers and Specialty Servers

Losing access to a shared resource can be costly in terms of downtime. Make sure that these resources are protected.

Tape Backup Systems and Tapes

If the wrong person has access to your backup system or tapes, you may be at risk of confidential data falling into the wrong hands. For example, a consultant in the Southwest who works with a large hospital was once offered $40,000 by a "headhunting" (personnel placement) firm for a backup tape containing personnel information. (*Author's note:* When the consultant told me this story, I said, "So what did you do with the money?") If someone less scrupulous had received the same offer, that tape could have fallen into the wrong hands.

Tape Storage. In addition to basic security concerns, backup tapes and disks have specific requirements that must be met if they are to survive long-term, archival storage. The *shelf life* (how long a tape can be stored and still retain data) of a tape can be affected by a number of factors. High humidity will shorten the shelf life. Dropping a tape cartridge on a hard surface can change the magnetic flux (the ability to retain magnetic images) of the tape, thereby shortening its shelf life. Another phenomenon is *magnetic print-through* or *bleed-through*. This means that the magnetic image from one portion of the tape bleeds through to another portion while the tape winds on its reel. Over time, print-through can degrade the magnetic image enough to make the tape unreadable.

Storage requirements vary with different types of media. Figures quoted by manufacturers are usually estimates, based on known properties of the tape, and should be considered maximums when tapes are stored under optimum conditions. In addition, if tapes are going to be stored for a period of years, they should periodically be rewound to avoid bleed-through. Shelf life can be effectively increased by periodically copying data from old tapes onto new tapes.

Off-Site Storage. Backup tapes should be stored off-site on a regular basis to guard against possible disasters such as fire, theft or earthquake. Probably the best approach is to contract with an off-site storage company, which will pick up tapes on a scheduled basis and store them in a temperature- and humidity-controlled environment that is protected against disasters. You arrange a regular rotation of tape exchanges with the company, and, depending on your contract, the storage company returns the tapes within a predetermined amount of time when you need to restore data.

Fire-Proof Safes. Unless specifically designed for magnetic media, so-called fire-proof safes do not provide sufficient protection because they are only intended to keep paper from burning. Unfortunately, tape and tape cartridges melt at a much lower temperature than the flash point of paper. In addition, fire-proof safes are rated for specified temperatures for specified periods of time. If a fire is hotter or lasts longer than the safe's rating, your tapes may not be protected. It may also take days or weeks to locate and open a safe after a fire.

Workstations

Several years ago, a student at George Washington High School in Denver, Colorado, installed a small TSR (terminate-and-stay-resident, or RAM-resident) program on a network administrator's PC that waited for the command LOGIN to be entered, then wrote the login name and password to a hidden file. The student was able to go back to the machine when no one was watching and recover the supervisor's login name and password, thereby gaining supervisor-level access to the file server.

This type of *Trojan horse* program is only one way that someone can wreak havoc on a system via a LAN workstation. Locally stored files can be read, modified or deleted. Even components can be removed. For example, one person attending a three-day seminar returned to find that someone had removed the video card from her PC! In another case, over a period of months someone removed as yet unused serial communications cards from dozens of PCs!

Of course, in most organizations it is not possible (or desirable) to lock up every PC, but awareness of potential problems is important. Some measures, however, can be taken:

■   Put PCs that store critical data in locked offices.

■   Some virus-checking programs will look for new programs or new hidden files. This can help locate Trojan Horses.

■   PC inventory programs can be used to discover new or missing hardware and software.

Shared Printers

A LAN administrator at a major bank once observed, "The company data processing auditors spend a lot of time on password security and access to sensitive on-line information, but they completely ignore the fact that all the network printers, where sensitive data is printed out, are in one room to which everyone has access!"

Make sure that printers used for sensitive data are located in a manner that prevents unauthorized access.

User Login and Authentication

As stated earlier in this chapter, security isn't just to keep the "bad guys" from doing bad things, it is also to keep us "good guys" from doing bad things accidentally. Typing "DEL *.*" while in the wrong directory may not be intentional sabotage, but it can still result in deleting critical files and data. By the way, an experienced, knowledgeable PC user is as likely to do something of this sort as a novice.

Life is not like the old Western movies, where bad guys were bad guys and good guys always wore white hats. Sometimes it's hard to tell them apart, and sometimes otherwise "good guys" do bad things. For example, when good employees become disgruntled or dissatisfied with their jobs, they can do things that are unexpected, disruptive and even disastrous to the company or organization. The stories of disgruntled LAN administrators changing supervisor passwords as they leave the company are all too common.

Unfortunately, LAN administrators in a great many organizations, large and small, take the attitude that everyone is trusted and competent, so security is not important. (*Author's note:* I have walked into numerous offices of large and small companies and government agencies where all users had supervisor-level access to the file servers.)

Proper login security and access control helps prevent both accidental damage and sabotage.

Passwords

Passwords are not the best method of authenticating users on a LAN, but they are the most commonly used method. They are easier and less expensive to implement and use than most of the alternatives, and are definitely better than no authentication method at all.

The biggest problems with passwords are that they are easily forgotten, easily learned by others and often easily guessed.

Unless proper precautions are taken, password security is easily broken. In the early 1980s film *War Games,* a teenage cracker[1] broke into a computer that controlled the U.S. missile defense system. Although the film was fiction (at least we hope it was fiction!), the techniques used are common. In the film, two programs were used—one to dial phone numbers and locate modem tones, and another to repeatedly try commonly used login names and passwords. These programs are easily available and also easy to write.

Things are not as hopeless as they seem, however. There are several methods that can be used to increase password security on a network.

Easy-to-Guess Passwords. To prevent passwords from being easy to guess, they should not contain:

- Any portion of the user's name
- Any portion of a family member's name
- The name of the user's pet or make or model of his or her car
- Any keyword of the user's job or function, like "entry" or "finance"
- Any known interest of the user, like "bicycles" or "49ers"

Forced Password Changes. Many network operating systems allow you to force users to change their passwords periodically. The major benefit of this is that if one user learns another user's

---

[1] *Authors note:* I use the term *cracker* here instead of the more commonly used *hacker* because it is more accurate. A cracker is someone who breaks into computer systems, while a hacker is someone who uses computers extensively for programming and other purposes. Unfortunately, this term is more often used, although inaccurately, to refer to computer criminals.

password, it will only be valid for a certain period of time, limiting the exposure to security breaches. On the downside, when people are forced to change their passwords they often forget them or write them down. When they write them down, they usually do so in a place that is easy to locate, such as a piece of paper in the top desk drawer, or taped to the front or side of their monitor!

If you are going to implement forced password changes, make sure that you keep the time periods reasonable. (Two days is probably too short, and two years is definitely too long!) Thirty days is probably a minimum, and 60 or 90 days is probably more reasonable in most circumstances.

Non-Dictionary Words. In his book, *The Cuckoo's Egg* (Pocket Books), Cliff Stoll recounts the story of a West German cracker who was breaking into U.S. Government computers and selling information to the Soviet Union. One of the methods he used for breaking into systems was to download a system's encrypted password file, then compare its contents with an encrypted English-language dictionary. If a user's password was in the dictionary, the cracker had access to that user's account. Although not all operating systems make it so easy to access their password files, it is still a good idea to have users avoid passwords that are in the dictionary.

Non-Alpha Characters. One easy way to create passwords that are difficult to guess, easy to remember and long enough to be difficult to break is to use two short words separated by a non-alpha character. Here are some examples:

WHAT?FOR
CLUB$TIE
GOOD%FRIEND
CROSS#STICK

Setting a Minimum Password Length. Passwords that are too short are easy to break, while passwords that are too long are difficult to remember. Obviously, then, passwords should be short enough to remember but long enough to be difficult to break. There are a couple of factors you should consider here, however. If you have implemented forced periodic password changes, you may want a shorter minimum password length. If you use the two short words and a non-alpha character approach, you might be able to get away with a longer minimum. In any case, a minimum length between five and ten characters should suffice in most circumstances.

"IT'S NO USE, CAPTAIN. THE ONLY WAY WE'LL CRACK THIS CASE IS TO GET INTO PROF. TAMARA'S PERSONAL COMPUTER FILE, BUT NO ONE KNOWS THE PASSWORD. KILROY'S GOT A HUNCH IT STARTS WITH AN 'S', BUT HECK, THAT COULD BE ANYTHING."

Password Encryption. There are two types of password encryption: passwords can be stored in encrypted format, and they can be encrypted across the wire. Both are important. When passwords are stored in encrypted format they are not readable by anyone, even a system administrator (see *Non-Dictionary Words*, above). This allows a user to use the same password on different systems without fear that the administrator from one system will learn the user's password on another system. Across-the-wire encryption means that the password is encrypted during the login process before it is sent across the network to a server or host. This prevents someone with a protocol analyzer from intercepting a user's password. Some network operating systems support one or both methods of encryption, and some support neither.

Supervisor-Level Passwords. If you have more than one user who needs supervisor-level access to a file server, give them each a supervisor-level account rather than having them share a supervisor password. This will give you a better audit trail and also makes it easier to change rights or a password for one person without affecting the others.

Written Password Policies. If you don't have a written password policy, you might consider implementing one. It should discuss the importance of maintaining the confidentiality of passwords and provide guidelines for selecting passwords. See *Appendix D* for a sample policy.

Time Restrictions

Some network operating systems let you set restrictions on what days of the week and times of day a user can be logged in. This feature is great for making sure all users are logged off the system for scheduled backups and maintenance. If you implement this feature, however, make sure there that you have a procedure to override it if users need to work during non-standard hours.

Intruder Detection and Lockout

Intruder Detection and Lockout, a feature provided by some network operating systems, will automatically lock a user account for a specified period of time if someone tries to access it with the incorrect password a specified number of times in a specified time period. The specific parameters are usually set by a system administrator. Intruder Detection and Lockout makes it difficult for someone to try a long series of passwords on a user account.

If you implement this feature, it is possible for someone with a list of system users (that means any user on your system) to force all accounts, including the Supervisor's, to be locked. This should be considered when setting the time an account should remain locked. You may also wish to create a second user who is granted Supervisor Equivalence. Then you can only be locked out if both the Supervisor and the second user are intruded upon.

Third-Party User Authentication Methods

There are a number of third-party user authentication methods available that can often provide additional levels of security. Available methods include:

■   **Tokens.** A token is usually a device that looks like a credit-card-sized calculator which generates a unique code every minute or so. The user must enter this code during the login process, and it must correspond with a code generated by the authentication system.

■   **Dongles.** A dongle is a device which attaches to a PC's parallel printer port. When used for authentication, if the dongle is not present, the user cannot access the system.

These methods usually rely on additional hardware, but they are generally expensive, difficult to implement and difficult to use. Many will only secure workstations. If they do provide LAN security, they are usually specific to a particular LAN operating system and may not help you secure access to all network resources.

Apple Macintosh

Apple's Chooser presents two serious potential security breaches. First, the Chooser allows a network user to embed her or his login name and password in the login screen so that she or he will automatically attach to network resources upon booting the machine. This means anyone using that machine has access to that user's network account. It is important to teach users not to put their passwords in the login screen. Second, the Chooser sends passwords across the network in unencrypted *clear text* format.

Novell provides an additional login and authentication method called the User Authentication Module (UAM). If you are using Novell's NetWare for Macintosh (version 3.0 or higher), you can use UAM to encrypt passwords and prevent users from using embedded passwords.

Concurrent Logins

Some network operating systems allow you to limit the number of stations from which a user can log in concurrently. Limiting a user's concurrent logins to one, for example, would prevent a user from leaving one logged-in workstation unattended while being logged in at another.

Station Restrictions

Some network operating systems allow you to restrict a user account to specific workstations based on the physical address of a network card. This can be useful in certain high-security environments. If a LAN card is replaced, however, the station restriction table will have to be modified.

Remote Connections

Remote connections can create a few additional security problems. Here are some tips to help you make your remote connections more secure:

- **Set modems to answer after four or more rings.** Most programs that dial numbers looking for modem tones will give up by then.

- **Select a dial-up number from a different prefix or out of order from the rest of your office.** If someone is looking specifically for a modem line in your office or company, they will try numbers that are similar to your voice line numbers.

- **Use callback features.** Callback means that the modem being called calls back the calling modem to actually initiate a communications session. Callback doesn't work for someone on the road who dials in from a hotel room, but it can add a level of security if someone dials in from a fixed location.

- Use proprietary software, such as PC Anywhere, Close Up or Remote LAN Node, for your communications. Since most crackers who are looking for modem lines use standard communications software, they probably will not be able to communicate even if they find your modem line.

- If you are using remote control software, force a reboot of the LAN station after a disconnection. This prevents unauthorized people from slipping in after someone else disconnects.

- Display a blank screen when a connection is made so the user has no clue what they have connected to. Under no circumstances should you put the word "welcome" on the opening screen. If you need to put up a screen warning unauthorized users about illegal access, don't make it the first screen displayed. This is a flag to crackers that there may be something interesting on your system.

Inactivity Time Outs

There are several products available that will log a user out from a network server after a specified period of inactivity. There is a major problem presented by this approach, however: determining what constitutes inactivity. Usually, these programs look for keystrokes. If someone is running a long database or accounting report, however, there will be no keyboard activity, but that PC could hardly be considered inactive.

Screen Blanking and Keyboard Locking

Blanking the screen and/or locking a PC's keyboard may be a better approach to securing unattended workstations than inactivity time out. There are several products available for DOS and Windows that lock the keyboard, blank the screen or both, and then require the user's password to unlock.

Guest Account Restrictions

Some LAN operating systems automatically create GUEST accounts. If these accounts are not needed, you should consider deleting them. Sometimes, however, they are used for functions such as multi-server printing, and in these cases they cannot be deleted. In these cases, the rights of these accounts should be restricted to the absolute minimum necessary to accomplish the needed functions.

Auditing

Some LAN operating systems provide the ability to audit certain kinds of LAN activity, such as server logins and logouts and file access. The only problem with auditing is that audit programs create audit logs. Even if you only want to view information occasionally, the audit log files need to be purged regularly or they tend to use excessive amounts of disk space. If you feel you need audit capabilities, implement them; but be aware that the log files must be maintained.

Access Rights and Logical Access Control

Access rights allow users to access the resources that they need in the manner in which they need to use them, while restricting access to other resources.

Directory and File Rights

Granting specific directory and/or file access rights to users and groups prevents unauthorized access to data and programs. The methods used and specific rights that can be granted vary with each network operating system.

Depending on your particular operating system, you can grant rights to files, directories or both. From a management point of view, it is a lot easier to work at the directory level than at the file level when granting rights. There are three primary types of directories to which you will be granting rights to:

- Private directories, such as users' home directories. In most organizations, users are given all rights to these directories to allow them to create, delete and modify files and subdirectories.

- Shared program directories. For these directories you will generally grant users the ability to read files and execute programs, but not the ability to delete or modify files and programs. This helps prevent accidental file deletion or modification as well as virus infection.

■ Shared data directories, such as directories for database files. For these directories you will generally grant the minimum level of rights necessary to access or update the data (as required), while minimizing the possibility of accidental file deletion or damage. Particular applications may force you to grant a greater level of rights than you feel is appropriate, however.

Directory and File Attributes

Attributes affect the way users can use files and directories. For example, a READ ONLY attribute says a file cannot be modified, deleted or copied over. Attributes should not be considered part of a security program unless users and programs are restricted from changing attributes. In addition, attributes usually have no effect on viruses.

Shareware

A lot of software is available through BBSes, information services such as CompuServe and the Internet. Most of this software falls into the categories of shareware, freeware and public-domain software.

Shareware is software distributed on a try-before-you-buy basis; if you like the product, you send the publisher money, and if not, you discontinue using it. Like commercial software, shareware is copyrighted.

Freeware, like shareware, is copyrighted, but the author provides it at no charge to anyone who wishes to use it, usually with the stipulation that it not be sold or used for direct financial gain.

Public-domain software is software that the author provides, often with source code, to anyone who wishes to use it.

Software is distributed as shareware, freeware or public-domain for a number of reasons:

■   The cost of commercial distribution, especially the cost of entry into the market, is prohibitively high for most small software developers.

■   Some useful utilities could not be priced high enough on the commercial market to be profitable to the author, publisher or reseller.

■   Some authors prefer this method of software distribution.

Shareware, obtained from a reliable BBS, on-line service or shareware vendor, is no more likely to cause security problems than shrink-wrapped software. In fact, many utilities that can enhance network security and reliability are available in this manner. There is also evidence to suggest that virus infection, one of the major reasons some companies cite for not using shareware, is more common from shrink-wrapped software than from software downloaded from BBSes or on-line information services. (See *Virus Prevention and Recovery* below.)

Data Encryption

As networks expand, the risk of sensitive data being read by the wrong person(s) increases. One method of dealing with this problem, in addition to standard file and directory access control, is encryption. Two types of encryption that can help secure data are on-disk file encryption and across-the-wire encryption.

On-disk encryption will make files unreadable by those who do not have the proper unencryption tool and/or password. Some applications will allow you to save files in an encrypted format, then require a password to unencrypt the file. There are also utilities available to do the same thing. Most of these utilities do after-the-fact encryption, encrypting an already existing file. The problem here is that there is a possibility that someone could access a file before it is encrypted. Saving a file to a local disk rather than a network drive before encrypting, however, can minimize that possibility. A related concern is the accessibility of temporary or overflow files that hold sensitive data. Usually these are not accessible by others on a network while they are active, but sometimes they can remain on disk in an accessible state if a workstation locks up or is powered down without closing files.

Across-the-wire encryption prevents data traveling across the network from being intercepted and read by the wrong person. Currently there are few across-the-wire encryption products, and most of those are hardware-based and expensive. Eventually, across-the-wire encryption will be a function of or add-on to network server and client software.

Virus Prevention and Recovery

Viruses are programs that attach themselves to computer systems and cause them to act in some nonstandard way. Viruses have invaded microcomputer systems in organizations large and small, public and private. They can do as little as display an annoying message, or as much as destroy all data on a disk. The variety of computer viruses detected so far numbers in the thousands. Viruses have come from areas as diverse as the United States, the Middle East and Eastern Europe. Viruses are common in the DOS, Macintosh and UNIX arenas.

The most common viruses infect the boot sectors of hard disks or attach themselves to .COM and .EXE files. Sophisticated viruses do everything they can to avoid detection. Sometimes   viruses display symptoms before they cause serious damage, but this is not always the case.

Viruses can enter a system in several ways:

■   Floppy disks. Floppy disks are probably the most common method of infection. In fact, boot sector viruses, one of the most common types of viruses, can only be transmitted directly between disks.

Floppy disks that have been known to transmit viruses include floppy disks from *shrink-wrapped* software, diagnostic disks carried by technicians from computer to computer, and shareware and public-domain software diskettes. Floppy diskettes carried from home and school computers, however, are probably the biggest culprits.

Shareware and public-domain software is thought by many to be the biggest culprit in virus contamination, but this is not true. Most shareware disk vendors and bulletin board operators are very careful about scanning software and disks before they are made available for distribution. The threat of virus infection is probably no greater from shareware than it is from shrink-wrapped software. In fact, the opposite may be true. Many software dealers have shrink-wrap equipment that they use to repackage returned software. The likelihood of virus infection from repackaged commercial software is much higher than from new shareware diskettes.

■   Modem connections. The popular view is that electronic bulletin board systems (BBSes) are hotbeds of virus contamination. Virus infection from reputable BBSes and on-line information services is extremely rare because their operators scan files and programs before making them available for downloading.

■   LAN-to-LAN connections. An extended LAN provides extended opportunities for infection. Implementing proper network security and exercising reasonable precautions will minimize this risk.

Virus Protection Software

An entire industry has developed that produces software to detect and eradicate viruses. Virus software is not all the same, however—there are differences in both what the software does and how it does it.

Virus software can do several things:

- Scan a workstation's memory for viruses. Some viruses will load into memory, then infect files.

- Scan a disk's boot sector. Boot sector viruses are by far the most common.

- Scan files on disk. File scanners can look for a number of things, including:

  - Characteristics of specific viruses, called *signatures*
  - Changes in files since they were last scanned
  - Files that are new since the last scan
  - Program files that exhibit anomalies, such as files with incorrect checksums[2]
  - Hidden files

- Scan files as they are opened or copied. This is similar to scanning files on disk, except that the scanning takes place each time the file is opened.

---

[2]A Checksum is a number computed based on the contents of a file or other data. Checksums are often used to check if a file has been modified.

■ Identify infected files and the particular viruses that are the cause of infection.

■ Eradicate viruses from boot sectors, files or memory.

■ Move or delete infected files.

No antivirus package can perform all of these functions, or at least perform them with all viruses. In addition, some packages are effective against some viruses and not others. Also, some virus software can produce *false positives*, erroneous reports of virus infection, with some files. Ironically, some packages produce false positives when scanning other antivirus software!

Antivirus software can be implemented in several ways:

■ Workstation executables that scan for existing files in memory or on disk

■ Workstation TSRs that can scan files as they are opened, disks as they are mounted and memory in both these cases

■ Server-based applications, such as NetWare Loadable Modules (NLMs) for Novell's NetWare, that can scan files on disk as well as when they are opened or copied

Most antivirus packages incorporate more than one of the above approaches.

Virus Tips

Here are some tips on preventing and handling virus infections:

■ Computer viruses must be considered a fact of life, like the flu or the common cold. Assume that at some point one or more disks will be infected and plan accordingly.

■ No virus package can protect you against all possible viruses. You may want to consider using more than one product.

■ Write-protect all original diskettes, working copies and boot diskettes before using them. This helps prevent those diskettes from being infected, and it gives you an audit trail for tracking the source of infection. (If you find that a write-protected disk is infected, there is a good chance that it is a source of infection.)

■ Maintain proper network security. Make sure all users have proper passwords, set access rights to shared directories to the minimum required, and, if you are a system supervisor, do not use a supervisor-level account for day-to-day work. (As a supervisor, you are probably more likely than others to infect your system with a virus, because you are probably loading more software than anyone else.) Fortunately, because the file structure of a network operating system such as Novell's NetWare or Banyan's VINES is different from that of DOS disks, many viruses that affect DOS disks cannot affect network volumes.

■ Use virus checking software to check files on server disk and workstation disks. Also check workstation disk boot sectors. Scanning should be done on a regular basis, perhaps as part of your backup procedure on file servers and daily when each workstation boots up. Server-based anti-virus software can schedule full server scans at any convenient time, such as the middle of the night.

■ Use software that scans files as they are being opened. The server-based products are very effective here since they don't use workstation RAM or processor resources.

■   Establish effective backup procedures. If you do have a major problem, you will probably need to restore files from backup. The backup procedure you establish will determine how quickly and effectively you can restore files.

■   Educate users about the dangers of viruses. Conscientious users are your first line of defense for virus prevention. Avoid scare tactics.

■   Use diskless workstations in high-risk environments. This method is effective, but it is not appropriate for all situations because it can also make it difficult for people to get work done, especially if they take work home.

■   Dedicated virus-scanning stations, used in a number of organizations, are not very effective. These are stations that users are supposed to use to scan all disks coming into the office. After a short period of time (usually one or two weeks), users will ignore the scanning stations because the procedure is time-consuming and troublesome.

E-Mail

The use of e-mail is creating a whole new set of issues for the LAN administrator and LAN user to worry about.

Some recent court cases have held that e-mail on privately owned computer systems is subject to the same rules of privacy as other forms of mail. On the other hand, operators of publicly accessible electronic bulletin board systems (BBSes) have had equipment confiscated by overly zealous law enforcement officials because of messages left by individuals on their systems.

Users may need to worry about audit trails. E-mail messages are usually backed up to tape during regular LAN server backup procedures. If your mail is sent through hubs, chances are that messages are backed up there, too. Archived e-mail messages played a big part in the Iran-Contra scandal. These were messages that had been deleted from computer systems but were restored from backup under court order.

It is becoming commonplace for lawyers to subpoena archived e-mail during the discovery process in lawsuits.. Poorly phrased or off hand comments could take on new, sinister meanings when viewed later in a different context. Those humorous faxes often sent between offices may now become part of the permanent record.

E-mail administrators and users alike must be aware of these issues. Court decisions and new legislation will probably affect you in this area. Policies and procedures regarding e-mail privacy and archiving need to be considered carefully.

Written E-Mail Policies

If you don't have a written e-mail policy, you might consider implementing one. It should outline your company's policies concerning e-mail access by other users as well as by management. It should also discuss both appropriate and inappropriate usage of e-mail, and the dangers of misuse. See *Appendix E* for a sample policy.

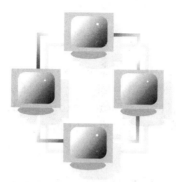

6

Backing Up Data

*W*e often find out that our backup systems or procedures are inadequate or unreliable only after a catastrophic data loss. Unfortunately, implementing a reliable backup system and procedures is not always an easy task.

In just a few years, LANs have moved from connecting a few workgroup computers to being the glue that ties enterprise-wide computing together. LAN file servers, and the data stored on them, have become as critical to the health of the enterprise as the minicomputers and mainframes that preceded them.

What Causes Data Loss?

Most data loss can be prevented, or its effects minimized, with proper backup systems, procedures, documentation and training. According to a 3M study, 60% of data loss is due to user error, such as accidentally deleting or overwriting or not saving files. Power problems, application errors, hardware problems and disk crashes account for much of the rest.

Backup Hardware and Software Requirements

Today's backup hardware and software is far more capable than in the past but is still far from perfect. Selecting a backup system always involves some tradeoffs, so you need to decide what hardware and software characteristics, functions and features are most important to you. Some of the major selection criteria are outlined below.

Backup System Performance

Performance can mean a lot of things. When applied to backup systems, it can refer to tape drive data transfer rates, backup or restore time for a given amount of data, or any number of other performance measures. Unfortunately, because of the number of factors that affect performance, quoted performance figures usually have little relationship to actual backup and restore times. Some (but not all) of the factors that affect backup system performance include backup system location (workstation or file server), backup device data transfer rate, effectiveness of the backup software, and network throughput and traffic load.

Some factors that on first glance would appear to improve performance can, in fact, impede it under certain circumstances. For example, if a computer system cannot supply data to or retrieve data from a tape drive at its transfer rate, a condition called *underrun* will occur. When this happens, the tape must stop while the tape drive waits for more data to be transferred. The tape drive must then reverse the tape to reposition it, then begin the read or write cycle again. Underrun causes excessive head and tape wear and degrades performance. This condition is also referred to as *shoe shining* because it causes a back-and-forth motion of the tape across the heads.

Figure 6-1: Intel StorageExpress Backup Server
(Courtesy Intel Corporation)

In most cases, a backup system attached to the computer it is backing up will provide better performance than a backup system attached somewhere else on the network. This means that a file-server-based backup system may provide better performance for the host server but not for other servers on the network. Backup systems running on client workstations usually do not provide the performance of server-based systems, but they are less likely to affect server operation if problems develop. Specialized backup servers that attach directly to the network, such as Intel's StorageExpress™ (Figure 6-1), are a compromise. They will generally provide better performance than workstation-based systems but poorer performance than a backup system attached directly to the server being backed up.

Like workstation-based systems, they are not likely to affect server operation if problems develop.

Speed of restore can be greatly improved by using a tape drive that has *quick file access* (QFA) mode. Most newer, high-capacity (1 GB and above) tape drives have QFA and can locate files on tape at speeds up to 200 times normal. This can mean restoring a file in a few minutes instead of several hours. QFA must not only be implemented in the tape drive, it must be supported by the backup software as well.

The only real measure of backup system performance is how well a particular combination of hardware, software and procedures works in your environment.

Reliability

To prevent data loss, you must have reliable backup systems and reliable, tested backup and restore procedures. Reliability means that your backup system provides error-free backups and restores. Accomplishing this requires a combination of reliable backup hardware and software as well as effective backup procedures. Problems caused by unreliable hardware cannot be fixed by software. Unless you have adequate backup procedures, chances are that at some point critical data will not be properly backed up.

Reliability is a two-part issue—data integrity, the ability to restore backed-up data, and hardware and software reliability, the ability of the system to function as expected. Today's tape drives are far more reliable than those sold a few years ago. They not only hold up better than previous models, but through the use of *error correction codes* (see *Error Correction Codes* below) they provide better data integrity as well. Software is also more reliable but is still the weakest link in the backup chain. Great care must be taken when selecting backup software.

Mean Time Between Failures. Manufacturers like to quote *mean time between failure* (MTBF) figures. MTBF means the average time for a failure to occur. Although MTBF figures can tell you something, they are usually a "best guess" estimate by the drive manufacturer based on estimated reliability of the components used. Some manufacturers perform tests that simulate accelerated aging, and this can help determine how a system will function in the field. Unfortunately, many backup systems are used at much higher duty cycles than they are rated for, often lowering the real MTBF. Environmental factors, such as temperature and humidity, can also affect the failure rate of a drive. MTBF figures are usually quoted at a particular duty cycle, meaning the percentage of time a device will actually be in use. Using a drive beyond its rated duty cycle can decrease reliability and cause premature wear. MTBF figures do not directly relate to recoverability of data from tape—they refer to proper mechanical and electronic functioning of the tape drive.

Error Correction Codes. Error correction codes (ECC) provide data redundancy on tape, allowing a tape drive to correct for or recover from media errors. The tradeoffs for this capability include somewhat lower performance and reduced effective storage capacity. Most newer high-capacity tape drives utilize ECC without software or user intervention. Vendors of the various tape technologies will provide evidence as to why their particular implementation of ECC is far superior to their competitors'. In practice, however, they all seem to do the job.

Tape drives using ECC perform an immediate read-after-write verification, rereading what it has just written. If what it reads is different from what it has written, it rewrites data to another area on the tape to correct the problem. ECCs detect and correct media errors but cannot do anything about errors caused by poorly written software, memory problems in a file server or workstation, network errors or hardware problems.

Head and Tape Life. Depending on the type of tape drive being used, the tape is sometimes or always in physical contact with the tape drive's read/write heads. Because of this, over time, debris and abrasiveness cause both the tape and the tape drive's read/write heads to wear. As tapes wear, the thickness of the magnetic coating is reduced, and the magnetic signal becomes too weak for the head to read. Tape wear is rarely even. The beginning of the tape usually experiences more wear than the end. If particular sections are subject to additional passes due to underrun, error checking or other causes, those sections will usually wear excessively.

Temperature and humidity can also affect head and tape life. High humidity increases the abrasiveness of the tape's magnetic coating, while low humidity can cause the formation of *friction polymers* which increase tape-to-head distance, reducing signal strength. The effect of temperature is indirect—as temperature increases, the allowable relative humidity decreases.

Without proper cleaning, deposits can build-up in the tape path and on the heads. This can increase error rates and even cause drive failure. If the build-up is too severe, even multiple cleanings may not remove them, and the affected drive may need to be returned to the manufacturer for repair. Tape quality can also affect deposit build-up. New tape formulations are helping to reduce this problem.

Maintaining Reliability. Here are a few things you can do to keep your backup systems operating reliably:

■ Monitor the number of times each tape is used, and replace or retire them early. Manufacturer's specifications on the number of times a tape can be used assume ideal conditions and tend to be highly optimistic.

■ Use the proper grade of tape. For example, video-grade 8 mm and audio-grade DAT tapes should be avoided.

- Tape drives should be used in clean environments, and temperature and humidity should be maintained within the specifications for the drive and media.

- Clean the tape drive and read/write heads regularly. Most drive vendors recommend cleaning after a certain number of hours of use. Some backup software packages will track drive usage and indicate when a drive needs to be cleaned. If yours doesn't, estimate usage (estimate high!) and clean accordingly. Make sure you use the proper cleaning cartridge for your drive.

- Perform test restores on a regular basis. (See *Backup Methods and Procedures* later in this chapter.)

- Verify your backups. If your software doesn't perform a true byte-for-byte comparison of files on tape versus files on disk, then change software or manually compare files on a regular basis. Unfortunately, a byte-for-byte comparison takes as long as backing up, but it is really the only form of verification that will tell you if your files can be recovered.

- Store backup tapes under the proper environmental conditions.

- If you are using tape for archival storage, test and rewind each archived tape at least once a year. Rewinding helps prevent *magnetic print-through*, the magnetic image from one part of the tape affecting another part while the tape is wound on the reel. Rewinding will slightly reposition the tape lessening this effect. If you are keeping tapes for several years, copy old tapes to new ones periodically.

Capacity and Backup/Restore Times

With high-capacity file servers, being able to properly back up within a limited time period is critical, as is the ability to restore a single file or an entire file server quickly. A backup system must be able to back up the required data in the time available for backup. With current technology, the most effective approach to backup for most organizations is to back up everything every day. The most effective time to back up is when all users are off the system and all files are closed. As server capacities increase, more time is required for backup. As server usage increases, the amount of time with all users off the system decreases. This means that faster backup systems, multiple backup systems and more efficient backup methods will be required.

Current tape drives have capacities up to about 5 GB, and data compression can, on average, double that. Many tape drives have built-in compression programs. This type of compression not only increases capacity, it can effectively increase the data transfer rate, since the data is compressed before it is written to tape.

Using multiple tape drives can decrease the amount of time required for backup. One way to do this is to have multiple backup systems running concurrently, each on a separate workstation or file server. Another approach is to use software that supports *parallel streaming*. Parallel streaming allows the backup software to read from or write to two or more tape drives simultaneously. A well-optimized system using parallel streaming can increase performance as much as 200%.

Job interleaving means the backup system can accept data from multiple sources simultaneously and send that data to a tape drive in an interleaved fashion. This approach, taken by GigaTrend's *MasterDAT*™ and Legato System's *Networker*™ backup software, can improve performance by keeping the tape drive's buffers full, thereby limiting underrun. It can, however, complicate the process of restoring files.

Tape changers can also increase capacity as well as help automate the backup process. They can also decrease the amount of time used by the backup process if they employ more than one tape drive (Figure 6-2).

Figure 6-2: ADIC Autoloader with Multiple Tape Drives
(Courtesy ADIC)

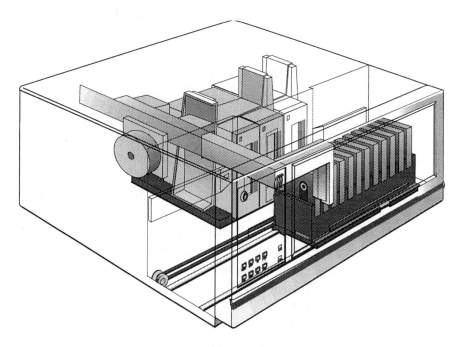

Ultimately, more sophisticated software will be needed to better manage the backup process so that full backups are not required. Palindrome's *Network Archivist*™ has gone a long way in this direction. The problem with partial backups is the amount of time required, as well as complexity of the task, of performing full system restores. Current software, combined with proper planning and procedures, can ease this process, but it is still overly time-consuming and complex.

In any case, it is a good practice to establish a period of time, or backup window, for performing backups. This should be a time when all or most users are off the system. In environments that require maximum up time, a short window can be agreed upon to allow a disk copy of critical data to another area on the file server. A disk copy on the server is much faster than backup to tape. With this method, the copied data can then be backed up, verified and logged by an alternate media, such as a tape drive, while the users are back on line.

Backing Up Open Files

Some backup systems will back up open files. This is fine for files that do not change, such as program files, but it can be a problem with data files, especially database files. The major difficulty is making sure that related files remain synchronized during the backup process. Effectively backing up open database files requires interaction between the backup system and the application.

First, the application must have a mechanism to allow files to be backed up in a stable state even when they are in use. Novell has provided this capability in the 6.x release of its *Btrieve* file manager (and *NetWare SQL*,™ which uses Btrieve), as has Oracle Corporation in it's *ORACLE Server*™ DBMS. Any backup system that supports Novell, Inc.'s *Storage Management Services*™ (SMS, discussed below) specification can backup Btrieve databases, with some manual intervention. Cheyenne Software's *ARCserve*™ can back up Btrieve databases automatically through the use of an add-on product called a *DBagent*™. *ARCserve* and Legato *Networker* provide similar capabilities for *ORACLE Server*.

Ease of Use

A poorly-designed user interface increases the probability of operator error. This can mean that critical data is not backed up or that current data is overwritten by older data during the restore process. Unfortunately, there are virtually no accepted standards or conventions for backup system user interfaces, so moving from one to another entails a significant learning curve. Good documentation, written specifically for your configuration, and proper training can go a long way toward reducing user errors.

Error Handling

Minor errors halting the backup process can be disastrous if they are not detected and dealt with. If you are performing unattended backups, it is important to select backup software that can continue operation when nonfatal errors are encountered. At a minimum, the backup software should provide an error log that indicates any problems that occurred during the backup or restore process and all files that were not backed up or restored and why. This log should be easily accessible to the backup system operator. In addition, a message should be sent to the backup operator when major errors occur. Some backup systems will send messages via e-mail, fax or pager to notify the appropriate parties wherever they are.

Security

To fully back up system and security files, backup systems usually need to have full, supervisor-level access to file servers and other network resources. This means that you will need to have some method of preventing unauthorized access during the backup process, especially during unattended backup. Most server-based backup systems provide this kind of security. Some, but not all, workstation-based systems also provide security methods. For those that don't, you may have to build a security system using tools such as public-domain keyboard locking software or other utilities.

Backup media must also be secured. The backup media has the same critical data as the file server, and access to backup data should be under the same security as in the on-line environment. Removable backup media, such as magnetic tapes and optical disks, should only be handled by authorized staff and stored in a physically secure area. Restore procedures should be secured as well.

Compatibility, Multiple Platform Support and Multiple OS Support

Although today's networks include client machines running different desktop operating systems, most backup software packages will only back up one or two file types. For example, Novell's NetWare 3.x provides support for DOS, Macintosh, OS/2™ (with the High-Performance File System, or HPFS), UNIX and OSI files. Most available backup systems can only back up DOS files from the server. A few can also back up Macintosh files, but there is very little available to back up the other file types effectively. Centralized backup of dissimilar clients is difficult, and may require multiple backup systems. Many products can back up DOS clients across the network, and a few can backup Macintosh clients and some UNIX clients.

Storage Management Services (SMS), a specification developed by Novell with the assistance of numerous backup system vendors, is an attempt to alleviate this problem by providing a method to back up multiple file systems on network workstations as well as NetWare file servers. SMS benefits users of Novell's NetWare, but little is being done to help users of other LAN operating systems.

When selecting backup software, look for the ability to properly back up and restore all files being stored on your file server and hosts, including system files and any extended file and directory attributes, file access dates, file and directory rights information, and directory size and volume trustee restrictions. The ability to backup multiple types of client workstations may also be desirable.

Unattended or Automatic Backup

Most LAN backup software can perform unattended backups. Server-based products usually have an advantage over workstation-based products in this area because security is usually easier to maintain on an unattended file server than on an unattended workstation. Workstation-based systems should be able to be run from a batch file or login script, which usually means that they must have a command-line mode.

Tape Cataloging

A tape catalog allows you to find a backed-up file or a version of a file even if you do not know which tape that file is on. This capability is provided by most LAN backup systems. As file server storage increases, finding out what data is on which tape becomes more important. If you cannot quickly locate and restore files from backup, end-user confidence can be significantly diminished.

Many backup software packages offer cataloging, but the capabilities vary. In some cases the catalog only provides a method of locating tapes by label, date or description, letting you then locate specific files once a tape has been selected. Some systems provide a complete backup history on a file-by-file basis, allowing you to easily locate and retrieve multiple versions of a file. Cataloging can have two negative effects on a system: it can affect backup system performance and use large amounts of disk space. The impact can vary widely from vendor to vendor. The file structure of the catalog and how it is indexed, as well as how well the cataloging program is written, will affect both update and access time. Long update times can tie up a backup station, while long access times mean longer file recovery times. If the application is poorly written, update and access times increase significantly as the catalog grows.

A number of products provide a feature called *automatic grooming*. Grooming means deleting files from disk after they have been backed up, freeing disk space consumed by little-used files. Automatic grooming is usually based on some aging criteria, such as the last-accessed date of a file. The process usually specifies that there must be a minimum number of backup copies of a file before it can be removed from disk. Usually, groomed files must be manually restored from backup when needed. This means that cataloging is nearly essential if you are going to find files that have been groomed. A number of products, including Cheyenne's *ARCserve*, Palindrome's *Network Archivist* and Intel's *Storage-Express*, provide this capability.

A more sophisticated approach to conserving disk space is file migration. This means moving files from one storage class, such as a hard disk, to another, such as tape, while providing an automatic return path. Novell has put the basic hooks for migration into NetWare 4.x, but its effective use will probably require third-party software.

Workstation Backup

Many LAN backup systems provide centralized backup of DOS workstation drives. Only a few, however, currently provide support for other clients. Novell, Inc.'s SMS (discussed above) promises to provide help for Novell customers, but little is being done for users of other LAN operating systems.

Backing up multiple workstation drives is time-consuming and requires the cooperation of users. If there are a large number of workstations to back up, it is difficult, if not impossible, to back them all up every night. In addition, most methods for backing up workstation drives provide very little security. They require that the workstation be running during the backup and, unless some sort of keyboard lock is employed, this means that anyone walking by has access to that workstation's data. The biggest problem, however, is enforcing the procedures that users must follow to allow the backup to take place, such as running the required workstation software and not shutting off their PCs. Given the current state of technology, it is probably better to encourage users to keep their data on file servers and make sure those servers are always backed up properly.

Backup Location: File Server, Workstation, Backup Server or Host

There are four common ways to connect a backup system to a LAN. All of them have advantages and disadvantages.

Workstation-Based Backup. The tape drive is attached to a workstation, and the software runs in that workstation when needed for backup or restore. Until recently, this was the most common approach, since most workstation-based backup systems have evolved from systems designed to back up stand-alone PCs. This approach has the advantage of simplicity. It is a lot easier to install a backup system on a workstation than on a network file server. Compared with server-based approaches, however, performance and security are usually weak. On the plus side, backup hardware problems do not affect file server processes or performance and components can be removed and replaced without affecting a file server.

A serious limitation of workstation-based backup is that file server backup speed is limited by the speed of the network, and is generally slower than with file-server-based systems. A file-server-based backup system can usually provide faster backup and restore for the host file server. This advantage is lost, however, when backing up other file servers. Another disadvantage is that the backup station must be logged in to the file server in order to back it up. If you are not careful, a workstation-based backup system can present security risks.

File-Server-Based Backup. The tape drive is attached to a file server, and the backup software runs in the file server as a server-based application. Server-based backup usually provides faster backup and restore for the host file server (the server to which the backup system is attached) than workstation-based systems. Also, scheduled and unattended backups do not require a user to be logged in at a workstation, providing a higher level of security than most workstation-based systems. If there is a problem with the backup hardware or software, however, that problem could affect other server processes. Much of the performance advantage of file-server-based is lost when you need to back up file servers other than the host. Also, a full restore would require the backup system to be reinstalled before files can be restored. Server-based backup systems lend themselves to centralized management more readily than workstation-based systems.

Dedicated Backup Server. The backup system is a dedicated unit with its own CPU. This approach provides independence from the systems being backed up. Unlike file-server-based systems, backup hardware and software problems do not affect file server processes or performance, and hardware changes can be made without affecting a file server. Unless the backup server has ties to a particular file server, as is the case with GigaTrend's *MasterDAT*, a file server crash will not affect availability of the backup system. This approach usually provides similar security to file-server-based systems. Performance will be limited by the speed of the network, but it is usually better than a workstation-based solution.

Host-Based Backup. Host-based systems use mainframe or midrange computer resources to back up LAN data. This approach, taken by IBM's *ADSTAR Distributed Storage Manager*™, Innovation's *FOR/UPSTREAM*,™ Legent's *ESM*™ and Network Systems' *USER-Access*,™ provides centralized backup and management. On the downside, costs can be significantly higher than with other approaches.

Backup System Costs

If you calculate the cost of reconstructing even one day's worth of data from one file server (if it is even possible to reconstruct), the the cost of a good backup system price is relatively trivial.

Even with the increasing importance of the data stored on LAN file servers, many companies balk at the $3,000 to $8,000 price tag of a high-capacity backup system. In fact, a good, high-capacity backup system, combined with sound procedures, can actually decrease the overall cost of backup. By implementing automated, unattended backups, labor costs can be kept to a minimum.

Backup Technologies

The most common medium for LAN backup and archiving is magnetic tape. Tape offers relatively high capacities (currently up to 5 GB per cartridge without data compression) and low cost. Other options, including optical drives and high-capacity removable magnetic disks, provide lower capacities and significantly higher media costs than tape and are not widely used for backup purposes.

Tape Technologies

There are four primary tape technologies used for personal computer and LAN server backup: *Quarter-Inch Cartridge* (QIC), *Digital Audio Tape* (DAT), *8-millimeter* (8mm) cassette and *Digital Linear Tape™* (DLT). Nine-track reels, widely used in mainframe and minicomputer environments, are rarely used in the PC environment. These technologies, in their current form, are all relatively reliable and all provide capacities of 2 MB or greater.

Quarter-Inch Cartridge (QIC). Developed by 3M and first sold in the early 1980s, QIC provides capacities of up to 2.1 GB and transfer rates as high as 600 KB/sec (kilobytes per second). Many early QIC drives suffered from reliability problems, and did not provide ECC. Newer large-capacity drives (525 MB and greater), however, provide ECC, QFA, and significantly better performance than earlier drives. Compression is also offered on some models.

8 mm Tape. Based on the 8 mm videocassette format developed by Sony Corporation and used in Sony camcorders, drives in this format are manufactured solely by Exabyte Corporation and their Japanese business partner, Kubota. Current drives have capacities of up to 5 GB (without compression) and transfer rates up to 500 KB/sec. A 20 GB drive, with a 3 MB/sec (megabytes per second) transfer rate, is promised shortly. Compression is also available on some models. All 8mm drives provide ECC, and newer models support QFA.

Digital Audio Tape (DAT). Designed for high-quality digital audio recording, DAT tape is 4 mm wide, and comes in a cassette that is similar to the 8 mm cassette but much smaller, about the size of a credit card. Capacity of newer drives is up to 4 GB, with transfer rates as high as 500 KB/sec. Compression is also available on some models. All DAT drives provide ECC and support QFA.

Digital Linear Tape (DLT). Although not as widely known or used as other formats, DLT, manufactured by Digital Equipment Corporation, provides capacities up to 6 GB and a transfer rate of 800 KB/sec. A 10 GB drive, with a 1.5 MB/sec transfer rate, is promised shortly. All DLT drives provide ECC and support QFA.

Grades and Types of Media

There is a lot of confusion concerning the difference between *data-grade* and *non-data-grade* 8 mm and DAT tapes. Much of the confusion, unfortunately, has been promulgated by the tape drive vendors and media manufacturers themselves. Non-data-grade tape refers to audio-grade DAT and video-grade 8 mm. Are data grade and non-data-grade tapes different? Some media manufacturers say "Yes" and some say "No." In fact, you can often get both answers by talking to different people within the same company. According to a product manager at Sony Corporation, Sony's data-grade media is different from their audio-grade media, meaning there are actual differences in the tape formulation. According to a Maxell engineer, their data-grade and audio-grade tapes "use the same high-quality media" (his words). Tape is made in wide rolls, then sliced. Some vendors say that data-grade tape always comes from the center of the roll, where the coating is generally more consistent. Data-grade tape may be subjected to more rigorous testing than audio- or video-grade tape. You should be aware, however, that testing is done by sampling—each individual cartridge is not tested. In any case, the difference in cost between audio-grade and data-grade DAT tapes is minimal. If you value your data, stick with data-grade tapes. The same holds true for cleaning cartridges. We have no hard evidence that cleaning cartridges for audio and video applications are different from those sold for data applications. It is best to be safe, however, and stick with cartridges designed for data drives.

Selecting a Backup System

It is beyond the scope of this book to review or recommend specific backup products or approaches. The proponents of the various tape technologies argue the merits of their favorite systems with an almost religious fervor. This often makes it difficult for the user to sort out the reality from the marketing hype. Your best sources of information are product reviews in the trade press and recommendations from satisfied users. Be aware that product reviews usually don't tell you how a particular product will work in your environment. Reviewers usually do not work with backup products in a real-world, production environment, and they often focus on the bells and whistles rather than the substance of the product. Reviews usually show products in the best, rather than the worst, circumstances, and rarely reflect how a product will function in case of a major data disaster. To get recommendations from other users who have had experience with backup products, find the closest network user group, attend a few meetings and ask about the experiences others have had. Make sure to talk to people who have had to use their backup systems to recover from major and minor data losses. On-line information services, such as CompuServe and the Internet, are also good places to find other users willing to share their experiences. Artisoft's ARTISOFT, Banyan's BANFORUM and Novell's NETWIRE forums on CompuServe, for example, are good sources.

© Joe Troise and Phil Frank

Backup Methods and Procedures

A strategy of consistent backup methods and procedures help eliminate guesswork in an emergency. When combined with good documentation, your backup approach should assure that critical data is properly backed up and that data can be recovered when and if needed. Your plan should take into account the time and effort it will take to restore data—as well as the complexity of the task—in a worst-case situation.

In addition to the above, you need to document your backup and restore procedures. The documentation should be written so that it can be read and used by a nontechnical person. You should also have it reviewed and tested (tried) by someone who does not know your backup process or backup system. This document should be short and to the point, covering the basic procedures used in your organization. It should, however, be detailed enough to cover such things as how to turn on the tape drive (if necessary), how to put a tape in the drive, and how to determine which tape to use. Assume that at some point in time backup or restore procedures will need to be performed by someone with little or no experience.

One final point—you need to test your backup system on a regular, scheduled basis. Unfortunately, there really is no good way to fully test a backup system, short of deleting all files and then restoring them (a rather dangerous practice!). The following approach will provide a reasonably good substitute:

■   Set aside an area on a file server for test restores.

■   Restore representative files of different types to the restore area. Test them by doing file compares with the originals using the DOS COMP command (for DOS files), which performs a byte-for-byte comparison. No errors should occur. If they are program files, make sure they execute. If they are data files, make sure they can be opened properly by their applications.

Make sure all attributes and file dates are properly restored, including any extended attributes and dates specific to your network OS, such as NetWare's Shareable attribute and Last Accessed, Last Archived and Last Modified dates.

Backup Cycles

Full Daily Backups. Back up all files, programs and data every day. This approach makes it easy to perform full restores or restore the most recent versions of files because all files on the last tape set are the most current. This approach also uses more time and backup media than other approaches.

Incremental Backups. Backup all files once a week and on a daily basis back up only those files that have changed since the last backup. If you need to do a full restore, it will require that you go back to the last full backup and then restore each partial backup in order, making restoring a slower, more complex process than restoring from full backups. Also, when you perform a full restore, files deleted since the last full backup will also be restored. This method can be used if you have time constraints or use expensive media (such as optical disk). Differential backups, outlined below, might be a better choice.

Differential Backups. Back up all files once a week and on a daily basis back up only those files that have changed since the last *full* backup. This approach means that a maximum of two tape sets will be required to perform a full restore. As with incremental backups, files deleted since the last full backup will also be restored.

Selective Backups. Back up only specific files and directories on a regular basis. One approach to this is to back up data files on a regular basis and program files only when changes occur. This approach only works in an environment that is tightly controlled. The problem with this approach is that program files do not get backed up as soon as changes are made, causing severe problems when files are restored. For example, files created with an upgraded application, such as a word processor, might not be readable by an earlier version. If you restore the older version, recently-created documents will not be able to be edited. Use this approach only if you can absolutely assure that the program files will be backed up when they are changed. By the way, make sure that menus, batch files and login scripts are also backed up.

More Frequent Backup Cycles. In some environments, more frequent backup is required. There are several approaches you can use. One method is to back up specific directories or changed files every hour or two, or even every few minutes. Another approach is called *journaling*. This means that the application writes database changes and updates to a separate file. This file can be used to rebuild the database if it somehow becomes corrupted or otherwise damaged. Journaling must be supported by the application. For the highest level of fault tolerance, it is a good idea to write the journal files to a file server other than the one that contains the database.

Media Rotation Methods

Media rotation methods let you use the minimum number of media sets needed to provide sufficient redundancy of backup. Depending on the needs of your organization, you may need more or less redundancy than the methods outlined below provide.

No Media Rotation. With the cost of DAT and 8 mm media well below one cent per megabyte, it sometimes makes sense to use a tape once and put it on the shelf. This will give you the ability to recover data from virtually any day.

Grandfather, Father, Son (GFS). GFS, the most commonly used rotation method, works as follows:

■   Backups are performed every working day of the week. Each daily backup should be on a separate tape. If the backup cycle is based on a five-day work week, you will need four daily tapes (we will discuss the fifth tape shortly). These backups can be full, incremental, differential or selective.

■   On the fifth day, a weekly tape is used. You will need three weekly tapes.

■   In the fourth week, a monthly tape is used. Since there are 13 four-week cycles in a year, you will need to have 13 monthly tapes.

When using this method, you must remember that the daily tapes are used most often and will probably need to be replaced soonest. If you are using off-site storage for tapes, you should either be equipped to create copies of your backups for off-site storage or set up a separate backup cycle for this purpose. If you are using backup tapes for archival storage, decide on an archive schedule (weekly, monthly, quarterly), and pull tapes from the rotation cycle accordingly.

Tower of Hanoi. This method uses each tape set a different number of times. Each time a new tape set is introduced to the rotation scheme, it is used every other rotation. Other tapes in rotation will be used every fourth rotation, every eighth rotation and so on. This is the primary method used by Palindrome's *Network Archivist* (see Figure 6-3).

Alternate Media and Milestone Backups. To be safe, never trust your backup system too much. You might want to back up critical files to different media on a regular basis. Critical files (those that cannot be reconstructed or restored from original diskettes) should he backed up to alternate file servers, local hard disks, optical disks or alternate tape drives as insurance against a catastrophic tape drive or media failure.

Milestone backups are backups that are performed before and after potentially dangerous or important events, such as accounting year-end reports, software upgrades or office moves. When performing milestone backups, you might want to perform alternate-media backups of critical files as well.

Figure 6-3: Palindrome's *Network Archivist* Tower of Hanoi Weekly Rotation Plan

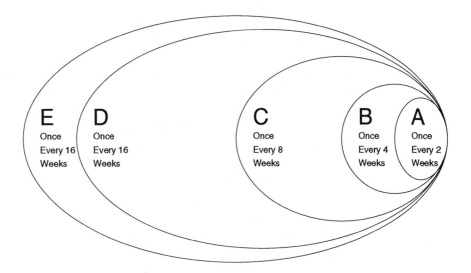

Off-Site Storage. Storing backup tapes off-site is an absolute necessity if you plan to recover after a major site disaster, such as a fire or an earthquake. Copies of original software should also be stored off-site. The best approach here is to contract with an off-site storage company,[1] which will pick up your tapes on a regular schedule and store them in a protected environment. Another approach is to exchange tapes with another office of your company.

---

[1]Several off-site storage companies are listed in the *Disaster Recovery Yellow Pages*. See Appendix F for more information on this guide.

Some companies store their backup tapes in a safe deposit box. This is a dangerous practice for the following reasons:

■ Access is limited to banking hours.

■ Only specifically authorized people, who must have keys, can have access to the box. If none of those individuals are available, or if the key is lost, access will be difficult.

■ In the event of a disaster, such as a fire or earthquake, access could take days, weeks or months.

In smaller companies, network managers sometimes take tapes home for safe keeping. You should have definite concerns about the security aspects of this approach, and you better hope that individual does not go on an extended vacation to a remote area without making sure someone else knows where the tapes are and has access to them.

Fire-Proof Safes. Most so-called fire-proof safes do not provide sufficient protection because they are only intended to keep paper from burning. They do this primarily by keeping oxygen out to avoid combustion, not by keeping the temperature down. Unfortunately, tape and tape cartridges can easily melt in such a safe at temperatures that paper can easily survive. Even if the safe is rated for magnetic media, read the fine print—a fire-proof safe is rated for a specified temperature for a specified period of time. If the fire is uncooperative, and burns hotter or lasts longer than the rating, you may be in trouble. It could also take days or weeks after a fire before you can get to the safe.

Data Recovery

Data recovery must usually be done under the worst of circumstances: a server hard disk has crashed, and everyone is waiting for it to be restored, or someone on a deadline accidentally deleted critical files. If you are going to be consistently successful at restoring data, you need to have a written, tested backup and restore plan. You also need more than one or two people trained in doing backups and restores.

Full system restores require a few extra steps. You must make sure that all of the files necessary to restore the system, such as original operating system files, are immediately available. You must also have your backup software available in order to restore data. You need to plan the restore process, especially if the possibility exists that you will be restoring to a different hardware configuration. Make sure you know what should and should not be restored, and make sure that information is part of your documentation.

For added insurance, it is a good idea to run reports of your file server's logical setup, including user and group accounts, security structure and trustee rights, just in case you need to reenter this information manually.

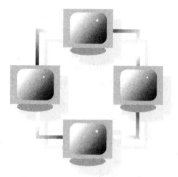

Power Backup and Conditioning

7

*F*or some unknown reason, your PC locks up, forcing you to reboot. Your network file server suddenly stops, and the console displays a message referring to "General Protection Interrupt" or "Non-Maskable Interrupt" fault. For a brief moment the lights dim, and your PC's screen "shrinks." A database file is mysteriously corrupted. A PC's power supply fails for no apparent reason. Your PC inexplicably loses connection with a file server.

All of the above problems could be caused by power disturbances and defects. Unfortunately, many of them can have other causes as well, making troubleshooting difficult at best. Nearly all LAN administrators are aware of the havoc that power problems can wreak on their systems, but most of us have little understanding of what causes such problems and how to deal with them when they occur.

Power problems are very complex, and the industry tends to give us simplistic solutions (i.e., all power problems can be solved with a surge suppressor, a UPS, or both.) In addition, very little independent information is available on the topic. Most research in this area is conducted or commissioned by vendors of power protection products, and each study almost always shows how that vendor's products or approaches to power protection are superior to those of the competition. The little independent research that has been done has dealt with single computers or centralized computer systems, not LANs. The distributed nature of LAN-based systems adds greatly to the complexity of the situation. In addition, LAN-based systems can be subject to power defects that usually will not affect stand-alone or centralized systems.

One thing is certainly true: If you are connected to commercial power lines, you will at some point experience some kind of power-related problem. The questions are, what kinds of problems will you encounter, and how do you deal with them?

You should be aware that the likelihood of a particular type of power disturbance has no relation to the damage that can be done if that disturbance were to occur. For example, Florida is considered by many to be the lightning capital of the United States, but lightning occurs everywhere. A lightning bolt striking a telephone pole in California can wreak as much damage as it would in Florida. In fact, it is often more damaging in areas where it is less common because people are usually less prepared for it.

This chapter attempts to give an overview of the kinds of power problems that you face and some possible solutions to those problems. When reading this chapter, you should be aware of at least four things:

1. The topics covered could be the subject of several books (at least two of which are listed in Appendix F).

2. There is a lot of controversy in the industry about power problems and appropriate power protection devices to solve those problems.

3. It seems that with many vendors of power protection products, the truth is not allowed to get in the way of sales and marketing. The phrase *caveat emptor* (Latin for "let the buyer beware") has probably no greater application than here.

4. The information provided here applies to the United States. Since other countries use different power distribution systems, some of this information may not apply to them.

Origins of Power Defects

Power defects (or *disturbances*, *interference* or *transients*) can have many causes. Lightning is an obvious source. Lightning does not have to hit power, telephone or data lines directly to affect electronic equipment. The electromagnetic field generated by a "near miss" can induce transients on these lines. As lightning current spreads into the ground, it can create differences in voltage at different grounding points and could possibly induce surges through the electrical grounding system.

The power company switching from one source of power to another can also cause defects to occur, as will the overloading of power circuits during heavy usage periods. Other sources of disturbance outside the building include downed power lines, causing outages, or lightning-induced *flashover* between power lines, causing momentary sags. In addition, heavy equipment outside your building can also create power disturbances that can be transmitted into your building.

Most power defects, however, are generated within the building. Copiers, electric motors, elevators, refrigerators, space heaters, arc welders, medical equipment, computers, cellular telephones and almost all electronic equipment are potential sources of power disturbances.

Potential Power Problems

There are several kinds of power defects that can affect your LAN and its components, as well as several avenues through which those defects can be induced. Power defects can enter a system via power lines, telephone lines, wide area network connections or even the LAN cabling system. Power defects that can cause problems include:

Power Outages and Blackouts. This means that the power goes out entirely. This will cause loss of any data in a computer's memory that is not written to disk. Some applications are particularly sensitive to this, and require extensive rebuilding of data files. Corrupted database index files are also common. Network file servers can be particularly vulnerable to power outages because file allocation tables, directories, cached files and system tables are often held and updated in memory. Power outages are most commonly caused by downed power lines, overloaded circuits in a building, the failure of power transmission equipment, power cords accidentally being unplugged or equipment accidentally being switched off.

Brownouts. In a brownout, the power will dip below normal for an extended period of time, meaning more than a few seconds. Persistent brownouts can cause data corruption and loss, and can cause computer power supplies to overheat and burn out. Brownouts are usually caused by the demand for power exceeding the power company's ability to supply it, but can also be caused by poor wiring system design within a building or chronic overloading of a building's electrical system.

Sags. A sag is a momentary drop in voltage. Sags can cause screen *shrinking*, RAM problems (often manifested as General Protection Interrupt [GPI] and Non-Maskable Interrupt [NMI] errors on file servers), and can also cause computers to reboot. Sags can be caused by problems in the power generation and distribution system. More commonly, however, they are caused by equipment within an office building, such as air conditioners, copiers, laser printers and electric motors.

Dropouts. A dropout is a total loss of power, usually under one second. Dropouts are often caused by utility switching.

Swells and Over-Voltage. These are sustained increases in voltage over normal. These problems are rare, and are usually caused by power generation and distribution problems. Over-voltage conditions can damage equipment.

Surges. A surge is defined by ANSI and the IEEE as "a transient wave of current, potential or power in an electrical circuit." This definition is somewhat broad—in practice, a surge is usually considered to be a momentary increase in voltage lasting between a few microseconds to a few seconds. These can be from a few volts to over 5,000 volts, with current up to thousands of amps. Surges of 50 volts or more are common, sometimes occurring several times per hour, while surges of over 1,000 volts are infrequent.

Most PC power supplies can handle *normal mode* (discussed later in this chapter) surges up to 600-1,000 volts (although there is no guarantee that this is true with all power supplies). Higher-voltage surges, however, can damage a PC's power supply or other components.

Spikes. Also called an *impulse*, a spike is a sudden, high-frequency (usually 10-20 kHz and above) increase in voltage. Spikes can be generated by lightning, or faulty or poorly designed electrical or electronic equipment. Spikes can cause sporadic disturbances, such as incorrect characters appearing on a screen, GPI or NMI errors, and can damage equipment. Spikes are usually low-energy disturbances.

Noise. Noise is unwanted, high-frequency (10-20 kHz and above) signals, usually generated by lightning, copy machines, air conditioners, elevators, refrigerators and switching power supplies (as used in PCs and newer fluorescent lights). Noise can cause sporadic disturbances, such as data loss and RAM and CPU errors. In LAN environments, noise has been blamed for mysterious intermittent glitches, such as a workstation losing communication with a file server for no apparent reason.

Static Electricity. High-voltage, high-frequency electrical discharges between objects. Static can cause mysterious, unexplained glitches, data loss, loss of LAN communication and chip damage. The failures caused by static are difficult to distinguish from those caused by other electrical transients. Static, however, will often cause keyboard or keyboard controller failures.

Ground System Defects. Electrical safety requires an "earth" ground; that is, a connection to a metal post or other metal object stuck into the earth, which can draw unwanted current literally into the ground, protecting people from electrical shock. For computer systems, grounding can also serve two other purposes:

■   To provide a "reference" point to compare a computer's logical, binary 1 (a +5 volt pulse) to its logical, binary 0 (a 0 volt non-pulse), called a *reference ground*

■   To provide a means to discharge static electricity, surges and spikes without damaging equipment

Unfortunately, these goals can sometimes work at cross purposes. An optimal grounding system for protecting people is not always optimal as a reference ground. It is important to note that an earth ground is not an electrical "cesspool" that just absorbs all electrical energy thrown at it. It is simply an electrical path and, depending on soil conditions and other factors, not always a very good one.

An electrical ground is made at a single point in a building, usually at the entry point for electrical service. If multiple grounding points are established, soil and other conditions can cause voltage differentials between grounding points. These differentials can create electrical hazards, affect the operation of network equipment and actually damage components.

Electrical resistance (or more accurately, for alternating current, *impedance*) can increase with the distance from the grounding point. This, along with other factors, can cause changes in the reference ground at different points in the grounding system. Some centralized data centers have a grounding grid, which is a mesh of ground connections, raised floors, chassis grounds and so on, all connected to the building's structural steel frame, providing an effective, single reference ground *within the data center*. With distributed LAN-based systems, however, this is virtually impossible.

Diverting any kind of energy into the grounding system can cause errors. Using the ground to discharge static and spikes momentarily induces electrical current into the grounding system. The static and spikes can change the electrical potential (voltage) between the ground and a component using it as a reference, possibly causing data errors. In addition, discharging static and spikes to ground can induce *common mode* power defects (discussed below).

Another potential problem is that the LAN cabling system can connect distant points in a building's safety grounding system (or between the grounding systems of multiple buildings), creating a complete circuit called a "ground loop." This can create:

■   A continuous current flow due either to electrical wiring problems, such as mis-wired electrical outlets, or differences in earth grounding systems. This is an especially common problem when LANs are cabled between buildings.

■   A momentary current flow caused by surges, spikes or noise at one or more points in the system.

Ground loops can, in effect, carry power defects into your equipment via the network cabling rather than the power lines. Some cabling systems are less susceptible to ground loops than others because all devices are electrically isolated from the cabling system. 10BASE-T Ethernet, for example, provides this kind of isolation, as will any fiber optic cabling system.

Ground loops can also develop between equipment connected by other types of cables, such as serial communications cables and printer cables. For this reason, it is a good idea to plug all equipment directly connected to a computer, such as printers and modems, into the same power strip.

Normal Mode and Common Mode

Power defects (on power lines) can be classified as normal mode or common mode. Normal mode defects are those that occur between the two current-carrying wires, called *neutral* and either *hot* or *live*. Common mode defects occur between the third wire (the safety ground wire) and either the neutral wire or the hot wire. Since the ground and neutral wires are (or should be) connected at the power entry point to the building, common mode defects are usually induced by equipment within the building and are often aggravated by poorly designed or faulty wiring systems.

The question of whether common mode defects constitute a problem for computer equipment has generated a lot of controversy. One camp says that common mode defects bypass the computer's power supply and have unblocked access to the system. The other camp states that common mode defects cannot get around the power supply and therefore are not a problem. Although this issue is somewhat controversial, current evidence suggests that common mode defects should not be ignored, especially in distributed LAN-based systems. In addition, if common mode defects bypass the power supply, which by design provides some power protection, it would follow that common mode defects do not have to be as large or powerful as normal mode defects to affect the delicate circuitry of a PC. Unfortunately, most power protection equipment for PCs, including most surge supressors, ignore common mode defects.

Defect Size versus Defect Speed

According to some experts, the speed of a power defect (*edge speed* or *rate of change*) may be as important as the size of the defect. An analogy can be drawn between a bullet shot from a gun and a baseball thrown by a pitcher. Both can be destructive, but the faster bullet is likely to do more damage than the much larger, slower baseball.

Lightning

Electrical surges caused by lightning can enter a computer via virtually any electrical or electronic connection. Lightning can generate currents up to 270,000 amperes (amps), and voltages have been measured as high as 5,000,000 volts! At these voltages and currents, lightning can cause problems with power and communications systems without a direct hit. Lightning hitting the ground near a telephone or power pole, for example, can induce a surge on the lines.

A common scenario is for lightning-induced surges to enter one network-attached PC via a modem and telephone line, and then travel across the LAN to other equipment. A computer or other component does not have to be on for lightning-induced damage to occur, it just needs to be connected to the affected source. Unfortunately, most power protection approaches focus on power lines, not LAN or telephone connections. A few companies, however, do provide surge protection for telephone and LAN connections.

Building the Foundation

The first step in power protection is making sure that your power distribution system is basically sound. If you have any doubts, you should have your system surveyed by an electrical engineer who understands the requirements of distributed computing systems. The survey should look for:

■   Good overall power system design. As with your LAN cabling system, good design of your power distribution system can help prevent problems from occurring. Unfortunately, many power systems are poorly designed. Even if the power system was properly designed initially, poorly planned additions and modifications can cause trouble.

■   Compliance with the National Electric Code (NEC), or its equivalent outside the United States. Compliance does not necessarily mean good design, but it does mean that your power system is less likely to create hazards to people and property than noncompliant systems.

■   Compliance with local codes and regulations. Local codes vary and are often more stringent than the NEC.

- Properly wired outlets. Use a simple circuit tester, the type with three LEDs, to check every electrical outlet.[1] These are available from most hardware and electrical supply stores (Radio Shack has one for about $6, part #22-101). Improperly wired outlets, in addition to being dangerous, can cause a multitude of problems and are extremely common, even in newer buildings.

- Proper wiring of *dedicated* circuits. A dedicated circuit has its own direct connection to its own dedicated breaker at the building's distribution panel. A dedicated circuit with *isolated ground* has its own ground wire and goes all the way back to the power distribution panel without splicing or branching. Unfortunately, some electricians have been known to take shortcuts on these circuits. (More about dedicated circuits later in this chapter.)

Like your LAN cabling system, your building wiring should be well documented, with labels at the circuit breakers and a map of the wiring system. In addition, your scheduled maintenance procedures should include regular inspection of the electrical system. During this inspection, you should look for the following:

- Integrity of circuit connections, including wall outlets and distribution panels. Improper connections can create disturbances and are a fire hazard as well.

- Potential circuit overloading. Overloading a circuit will cause its breaker to trip, creating a power outage on that circuit. Most standard electrical circuits in the U.S. are designed to handle sustained loads of either 15 or 20 amperes (amps). Each circuit,

---

[1]These testers must be used properly. If equipment is plugged in to the circuit being tested, you could get false readings. Read the instructions before using the tester.

however, usually supports several outlets. In order to check for circuit overloading, it is important to have a wiring diagram that shows which outlets connect to which circuits.

■   Heavy loads. One or more heavy loads (equipment that draws a large amount of current, either continuously or intermittently) on a circuit shared by other equipment can exacerbate the problem of circuit overloading.[2]

■   Harsh loads. *Harsh* loads (devices that generate significant electrical interference back onto the power lines) and heavy loads should be isolated as much as possible from critical or sensitive electronic devices. Such devices include air conditioners, refrigerators, copiers, elevators and certain medical equipment. Placing these loads on dedicated circuits with isolated grounds can provide some degree of isolation from interference, but, because all circuits eventually connect together at the distribution panel, may not totally eliminate interference. (More on dedicated circuits below.)

■   Changes and additions that do not meet specifications. This includes improperly wired outlets and incorrectly installed "dedicated" circuits.

■   If you suspect that you have power-related problems, use a recording power quality monitor to check electrical power quality over time. You need one that will register impulses with peak voltages as low as 5 to 10 volts, and can record both normal mode and common mode events. These cost between $600 and $20,000 dollars, and can often be rented from

---

[2]A common problem is this: Some laser printers periodically turn their drums when they are idle. This cycling can draw up to 30 amperes of current for about one-half of a 60 Hz cycle. If three or four printers happen to cycle at the same time, an immense current draw can result.

instrument rental companies.[3] Be aware that such instruments can vary considerably in quality and capability.

Dedicated Circuits with Isolated Ground

A dedicated circuit with isolated ground can be identified by its characteristic orange outlet. Properly wired, a dedicated circuit connects to its own circuit breaker at the power distribution panel. In addition, a dedicated circuit must have two ground connections—one connecting the enclosures (i.e., the outlet box to the breaker box), and one connecting to grounding point at the building's power service transformer without touching any intermediate enclosures.

There are two major potential problems with these circuits: because there is much misinformation about how they are to be installed, they are often installed incorrectly; and they usually increase the ground path between the device on the dedicated circuit and the rest of the power system. Because of the potential for ground loops and other reasons too technical for this discussion, you are usually better off not connecting LAN equipment to dedicated circuits.

Neutral Line Harmonics

Switched-mode power supplies, the kind used in PCs, newer fluorescent lights and other electronic equipment, are creating a new electrical hazard in commercial buildings served by three-phase power, especially with wiring systems that use a shared or undersized neutral wire (something allowed by the NEC): these devices generate harmonics on the power lines that can overload the neutral side. These harmonics can actually create up to 1.73 times the current flow on the neutral line. Since circuit breakers are on the hot line, generally one of two things happen in this case: the service transformer supplying

---

[3]The power company will sometimes, at your request, provide a recording power meter to check for electrical problems. Generally speaking, these meters will not be sensitive enough to register fast-edged, low-voltage transients.

power to the building can burn out, or a neutral wire can overheat and start a fire. Modular office furniture, which commonly uses shared, undersized neutral wires, is especially at risk. Two things can happen: a neutral wire can overheat, causing a fire, or the pin-feed connectors on the electrical receptacles or the connectors between panels can fail, creating under- and over-voltage conditions that can burn out power supplies and cause other damage. This phenomenon has reportedly been responsible for a number of building fires.

There is some work being done to set power-supply design standards to help alleviate this situation, mostly in Europe. In fact, a new European Community regulation, IEC 555, will require power-factor corrected power supplies, which limit harmonic output, in new computers. In the United States, most of the effort is concentrating on power supplies for larger equipment. Unfortunately, large numbers of smaller pieces of equipment, such as personal computers and fluorescent lights, are often the biggest culprit in this situation.

There are no easy solutions to this problem, but the following can help:

■ Have your electrical system surveyed by someone who understands power harmonics and has the knowledge and equipment to test your power system for vulnerability.

■ Redesign the power system so that neutral lines are not shared and not undersized.

■ Replace the power transformer to the building with a type known as a K-factor transformer.

■ Use harmonically-compensated ferro-resonant transformers (discussed later in this chapter) on all equipment that has a switched-mode power supply.

■   Specify power-factor corrected power supplies on computers and other electronic equipment. These are now being shipped on some European models, but usually not U.S. models. Some vendors, however, may supply them by special order. They may also be available to retrofit existing PCs.

None of the above approaches should be taken without consulting a qualified professional first, and none of these approaches is inexpensive.

LAN Cabling

Fortunately, modern LAN cabling systems, including Token Ring and 10BASE-T Ethernet, provide a high degree of isolation between network components. Earlier systems, however, including Thin Ethernet coaxial cable systems, were often guilty of carrying power disturbances from one computer to another and were especially prone to ground loops. To minimize power problems related to LAN cabling, here are a few tips:

■   Make sure your network cabling system is properly installed. Cables running in parallel with power circuits or near fluorescent lights, large electric motors and so on can cause problems.

■   Choose a cabling system and network architecture that provide a high degree of isolation between network components.

■   Use fiber optics or other non-copper link (such as a wireless link) between buildings.

Power Protection Solutions

Because the causes of power problems are so diverse and the effects so difficult to determine, it is difficult to make generalizations about appropriate power solutions. In addition, there is some disagreement in the industry about the effectiveness of some power protection products.

Power protection efforts, however, generally fall into four areas:

■ Maintaining consistent AC line voltage

■ Providing backup power during outages

■ Protecting equipment from damage due to electrical surges and other interference

■ Protecting logic circuits and data from disruption due to electrical interference

Maintaining Consistent AC Line Voltage

Most computer equipment built since the early 1980s, including virtually all personal computers, use a type of power supply known as a *switching* power supply. Without going into technical details, suffice it to say that switching power supplies provide better voltage regulation than most voltage regulating devices. This means that external voltage regulating equipment is at best redundant in most situations. At worst, since voltage regulating equipment can also generate a certain amount of electrical interference, it can add to electrical problems.

Providing Backup Power During Outages

Backup power systems are used for two purposes:

■ To provide for the orderly shutdown of a computer system in the event of a power outage

■ To provide continued operation in the event of a power outage

Backup Power Supplies. The most common device used for power outage protection is a *backup power supply* (BPS).[4] The two most common types of BPS are *uninterruptable power supplies* (UPS) and *standby power supplies* (SPS). BPSes are generally used to provide short-term (a few minutes to a few hours) power backup, and provide immediate or nearly immediate power when outages occur.

Standby Power Supplies (SPS). An SPS contains batteries and a power "inverter," which can take the batteries' DC output and convert it to 120 volt AC output. Under normal power conditions, an SPS delivers power from the incoming commercial power lines. If incoming power drops (usually below approximately 100 volts), the SPS switches from the commercial lines to the batteries and inverter, supplying power to the devices plugged into them.

The downside to an SPS is that there is a small delay, or switch-over time, between the moment the power goes out and the moment the inverter kicks in; usually between four and six milliseconds. Power supplies in some older PCs shut down in less than four milliseconds, and some poorly-designed standby UPSes take longer than six milliseconds to switch in. In addition to switch-over time, there is the time it takes the SPS to sense a power outage. Some vendors include this time in their switch-over times, some do not. Some vendors state that their SPSes include surge protection or line conditioning (discussed below), but in many cases, especially with lower-priced units, such protection is minimal at best.

---

[4]Arguments rage over the proper use of the term *uninterruptable power supply* (UPS). Although commonly used to refer to all power backup systems, it technically refers to only one type of system. Therefore, this book will use the more generic term *backup power supply* (BPS) when referring to this class of power protection equipment.

Uninterruptable Power Supplies (UPS). An on-line (or full-time) UPS differs from the standby units in that its battery and inverter are constantly powering the attached equipment. An on-line UPS only resorts to AC power when the battery power is interrupted or fails. An advantage of on-line systems is that there is no switch-over time. UPSes, however, are generally more expensive than equivalent SPSes and generate more heat, and their batteries usually have shorter lives than equivalent SPS batteries. Some manufacturers of SPS systems criticize on-line systems by stating that commercial power is almost always better than that produced by a BPS (stand-by or on-line), and commercial power should be used when it is available.

Ferro-Resonant Standby Power Supplies. A *ferro-resonant* stand-by power supply adds a special transformer to the output of an SPS. This ferro-resonant transformer provides voltage regulation (unnecessary with PC power supplies) as well as a good degree of filtration and power-line isolation. Ferro-resonant SPSes are generally much bulkier and heavier than other units. Also, unless they are operated at full capacity, ferro-resonant systems are less efficient electrically (i.e., use more power) and run hotter than other units. Some competitors also criticize ferro-resonant transformers because they provide a high impedance output (see *High or Low Impedance Output* below) and can reflect noise back to the load being protected. Vendors of ferro-resonant systems counter by saying that a ferro-resonant system prevents noise from going back to the power line and that there is no specification for input impedance for PC power supplies. Also, some ferro-resonant vendors address these problems by installing high-frequency capacitors on outputs to take care of noise. According to one vendor of competing technology, there is one potential problem with power-factor corrected power supplies (designed to limit power-line harmonics) and ferro-resonant transformers: under some circumstances, the transformer and power supply can cause current to be drawn in an oscillating manner, causing large swings in output voltage and currents. Again, since there have been few independent studies, this claim is difficult to verify.

As the arguments rage over the "best" method for providing backup power, the user gets lost in the battle because there are few if any independent studies to validate or refute competing vendor claims. Vendors of all backup systems will argue the merits of their respective approaches. There seem to be good-quality units in all three categories and, unfortunately, poor-quality units as well.

High or Low Impedance Output. There is some argument over the effect of the impedance of the output of a BPS or other power protection device that uses a transformer, such as a line conditioner. Vendors of units with low output impedance say their units do a better job of absorbing noise generated by the load into the transformer (rather than reflecting it back to the load) than high-impedance devices. Vendors of high-impedance devices say that their units do a better job of preventing noise from being reflected back on the power lines and that noise reflection back to the load is not a major concern. Unfortunately, this seems to be an area where little independent research has been done, so it is difficult for the buyer to draw a conclusion.

Output Wave Form. The wave form of the current supplied by the backup power system is very important to the longevity of your equipment.

Backup power systems usually generate current in sine wave or square wave form. Commercial AC power is delivered in the form of a sine wave (see Figure 7-1).

With a sine wave, power changes gradually from a low of 0 volts to a peak of approximately +170 volts, falls gradually back to 0, then changes to a peak of -170 volts. The 120-volt figure that is quoted for commercial AC power is an average value, the RMS value.

Figure 7-1: Sine Wave

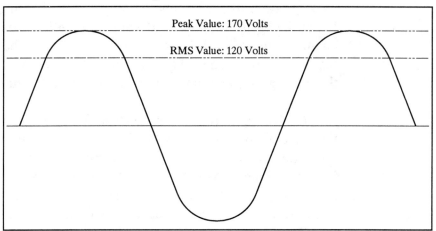

Peak Value: 170 Volts

RMS Value: 120 Volts

The 120-volt RMS value determines the brightness of light bulbs and affects transformers. Computer power supplies, however, generally use the 170-volt peak value.

Unlike the gradual change of a sine wave from a positive to a negative voltage, a square wave switches instantly from a positive to a negative voltage. With a square wave, the peak voltage and RMS voltages are identical (see Figure 7-2).

Because the internal power supplies in computers use the peak voltage, and lights and transformers utilize the RMS voltage, backup systems that have a square wave output usually compromise between 120 and 170 volts, commonly at 140 volts.

This means that the voltage is too low for computer power supplies, potentially causing overheating, yet too high for transformers, light bulbs and so on, potentially causing shortened life or burnout. This kind of compromise could be classified as the worst of both worlds. Also, depending on the kind of fan used in a computer, a square-wave output can slow the fan down, making the computer run hotter. This may not be a problem for a few minutes, but it could cause problems if the BPS operates for an extended period of time. When testing a BPS, check to see if the fan speed stays consistent when the equipment is running off the BPS.

Figure 7-2: Square Wave

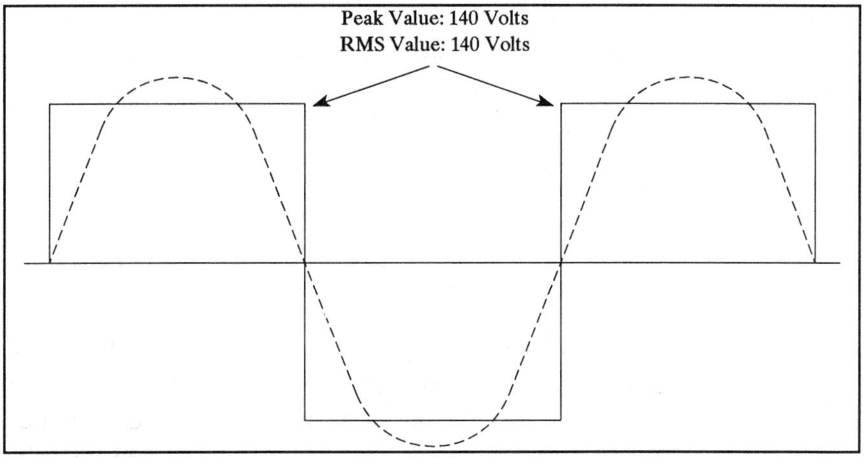

Peak Value: 140 Volts
RMS Value: 140 Volts

BPSes that generate square wave output are generally less expensive than systems that generate sine waves.

A third wave form, *quasi-sine wave* (sometimes called *pseudo-sine wave*), outputs a square wave that is "stepped" (see illustration) to approximate a sine wave. Generally, this kind of unit has most of the benefits of sine wave output but can be produced at a lower cost.

Two other wave forms need to be mentioned. These are the *modified square wave* and the *rectangular wave*. These wave forms are often generated by less expensive BPSes, and are generally better for computers than square waves but less desirable than sine waves or even quasi-sine waves.

Figure 7-3: Quasi-Sine Wave

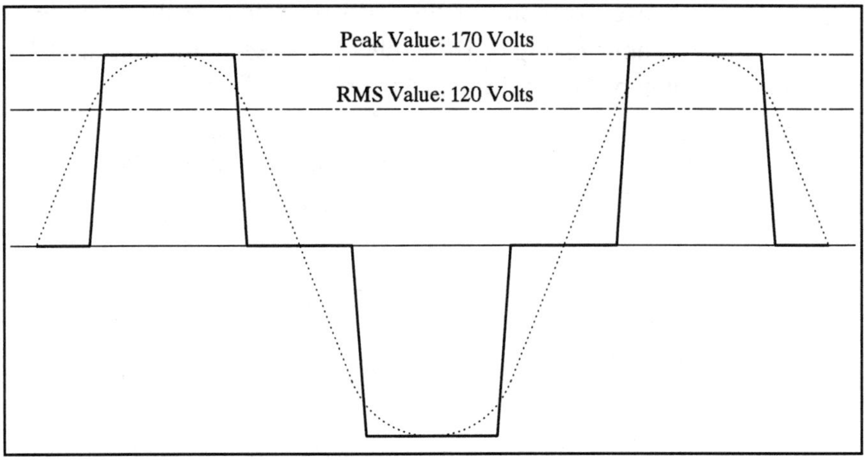

Peak Value: 170 Volts

RMS Value: 120 Volts

Rated Power Capacities. Power capacities of BPS systems are rated in watts or volt-amps (V-A). Larger BPSes are usually rated in V-A, while smaller systems are often rated in either watts or V-A. The two measurements, which are often used interchangeably, are in fact quite different.

For one type of electrical equipment, the watt and V-A ratings can be the same, while for another type of equipment they can be different. For example, for light bulbs and electric heaters, watts and V-A are equivalent values. For computers, however, the watt rating is approximately 60% to 70% of the V-A rating.

To add to this confusion, many manufacturers actually mean V-A when they say watt. The confusion of these terms can make it difficult to "size" a BPS for your network. Probably the best approach, short of learning more than you want to know about power, is to rely on the BPS manufacturers' recommendations with respect to size. Most manufacturers provide charts showing recommended units to be used with particular computers and/or peripherals. Before you make your selection, however, read the next section on battery life.

Battery Life. BPS batteries wear out, usually in two to five years. It is important to note that batteries usually don't wear out suddenly, unless they are defective. As they wear, their capacity for providing power will gradually degrade, and as they become nearly worn out, their performance will dramatically drop off.

As stated above, BPSes are rated as to how long they can provide backup for a specific current load. While most vendors are somewhat conservative on their ratings, you should be aware that the ratings are usually based on new batteries.

Many newer BPSes provide battery monitoring capabilities to let you know when it is time to replace them, but this will usually indicate that the battery is nearly worn out. To be safe, it is a good idea to use a BPS that is rated for at least twice the capacity that you need. Another approach is to use a BPS that allows you to add additional battery packs to extend backup time. For example, American Power Conversion (APC) has a model that allows you to add both batteries and power units as needed. If you take this approach, add enough batteries for double your required backup time. In any case, replace your batteries at least every two to three years.

Some BPSes make it easy to replace batteries, some do not. Some models, such as those from ONEAC Corporation, allow you to change batteries while the BPS is on line, and some do not. Some models need to be returned to the factory for battery replacement! Before purchasing a BPS, find out the procedure for replacing batteries. You should also find out where batteries are available and their approximate cost. If your BPS requires batteries of a proprietary design, you can expect the cost to be significantly higher than that of general-purpose batteries.

Testing a BPS. A common but poor test for a BPS is pulling its plug from the wall socket while it is powering equipment. This method creates an open circuit across the plug of the BPS. When power goes out in real situations, however, the load of all the other devices attached to the power lines creates a short circuit, rather than an open circuit, across the plug. Many BPS systems will pass the pull-the-plug test, only to fail when a real power outage occurs. Another problem with this test method is that it interrupts ground, which can create stray ground-related voltages that can cause problems. If you feel the need to test in this manner, use a switched power strip instead of pulling the plug. Unfortunately, however, there really is no good way to realistically field-test a BPS.

BPS Monitoring. Many backup power systems include the capability to send messages to attached equipment, such as a network file server, to indicate when commercial power is interrupted, when the BPS battery is low and so forth. This function is called, not altogether correctly, *UPS monitoring*. UPS monitoring allows a file server or computer to initiate an unattended orderly shutdown procedure.

To implement monitoring, a cable is connected between the BPS and serial port or a special UPS monitor board installed in the computer's expansion bus. Some operating systems provide built-in monitoring functions, while some require additional software. Some BPS vendors supply software with enhanced functions, even for operating systems that support monitoring natively.

If commercial power to the BPS goes out, the BPS sends a signal to the computer (usually a file server or time-sharing host) via the UPS monitoring connection, indicating a power outage. The server or host can then perform the actions its software specifies, such as sending a message to users that the power is out and that the server will shut down in a specified number of minutes. When a specified period of time has passed, the server or host will usually close all open files and shut itself down. If the power should be restored before the indicated shutdown time, the process will usually be aborted.

BPS Management. The *Simple Network Management Protocol* (SNMP), part of the TCP/IP protocol suite, is quickly becoming the accepted standard for network device management. BPS vendors are proposing a standard BPS extension, or *management information base* (MIB), to be added to the SNMP specification. This will allow BPSes to be monitored and managed across the network in the same way as other network components. A major benefit over simple BPS monitoring is that various activities, not just server or host shutdown, can take place in the event of a power outage.

Backup Power Generators. A BPS is used to provide immediate power in case of an outage, but only for a few minutes or a few hours. If backup power is needed for continuous operation, a generator is a good option. Generators are usually used in conjunction with BPSes for two reasons:

1. BPS batteries do not last forever, and switching to generator power allows you to reduce battery size and your reliance on the battery pack.

2. A generator must be turned on before it can provide power. The BPS can keep critical equipment powered until the generator is started.

The advantage of a generator is that it can provide power for as long as you give it fuel. Barring an equipment failure, this could be for hours, days or even weeks. If your power system includes a backup generator, good power conditioning is important, since a

generator switching on or off can create significant power
disturbances, and power produced by backup generators is generally
"dirtier" than commercial power. If you plan to use a generator in
your system, contact a good power quality consultant before you do.

Protecting Equipment from Damage and Protecting Logic Circuits and Data from Disruption

Until the 1980s, the major focus of power protection equipment
was to protect against downtime caused by power outages and
against damage to equipment caused by lightning-induced surges on
power lines and lightning-induced surges and stray electrical current
(called *sneak current*) on telephone lines. While these problems still
exist, very large scale integrated (VLSI) circuits, made by depositing
trace amounts of metal onto the surface of treated silicon crystals,
have created a whole new class of problems. VLSI circuits, the type
used in virtually every computer today, can be affected by much
lower currents and voltages than older equipment. A very small
transient voltage can physically damage a VLSI chip, or it can be
mistaken for a digital signal. If a transient voltage occurs in the right
way at the right instant, it can change a computer's instruction or
result in spurious hardware interrupts that can produce system errors
or lock up a file server or other computer.

This means that many problems which are blamed on software
or hardware failure may actually be caused by power transients.

Solving these problems is not always a straightforward
proposition, especially considering the lack of solid information
available and the conflicting data supplied by vendors. Adding to the
confusion is the possibility that disturbances can enter a system via
the power lines, modem connections or LAN cabling.

Power Supplies. As stated above, nearly all modern computers and peripherals use switching power supplies. Although characteristics vary, switching supplies for PCs have a few things in common:

■ Switching power supplies provide effective voltage regulation. Switching supplies generally provide better regulation than external voltage regulation devices.

■ Switching supplies all provide some level of surge protection. Whether it is sufficient to preclude the need for additional suppression, however, is the subject of much debate.

■ To meet government regulations in the U.S. and other parts of the world, most computer power supplies include some form of filtration for radio frequency (RF) interference. Although this filtration is designed to prevent noise from being broadcast onto the power lines, it also provides some filtration of incoming noise. These filtration circuits, however, can only be guaranteed to be effective against the type of noise generated by that power supply and those circuits, not against noise with different characteristics. In addition, if the incoming noise contains more energy than the filtration circuit was designed to control, the circuit could "saturate," thereby neutralizing its effectiveness.

Even though a computer's power supply provides some level of protection, power disturbances still seem to find a way through or around it to affect the rest of the system.

Power conditioning equipment generally falls into one of the following categories.

Surge Suppressors. Surge suppressors are the most widely used type of power protection device in the United States.[5] Surge suppressors are designed to protect against momentary voltage surges and spikes. Surge suppressors vary greatly in both price and capability, and often, it seems, the two are not related. The least expensive surge protectors use a simple device called a metal oxide varistor (MOV), or a slightly faster-acting device called an *avalanche diode* or *zener diode*. MOVs and zener diodes are *shunt* devices and basically divert surges and spikes, usually to the neutral line, but some high-end surge protectors use multiple MOVs or zener diodes to attempt to divert surges equally between hot, neutral and ground. These devices have limited energy-handling capabilities and, when used by themselves, can be destroyed by surges over time. Although one vendor of competing equipment calls them "sacrificial" devices, most catastrophic failures are usually caused by poor design or extremely powerful surges. Some, but not all, surge protectors include some type of mechanism to indicate that the protector has failed. Unfortunately, there is no good, *nondestructive* field test that can be performed on these devices to assure that they work. Some MOV or diode failures can cause fires, so it is a good practice (and a legal requirement in some areas) to make sure that the protector has a UL label.

Some medium-priced surge supressors use other devices in addition to MOVs and zener diodes. Gas discharge tubes divert large amounts of surge energy and are often used to divert surges that overcome other surge devices. In addition, the better suppressors include some level of electromagnetic interference/radio frequency interference (EMI/RFI) filtration.

---

[5]***Author's Note:*** This is not necessarily true in the rest of the world. For example, I recently conducted a LAN management seminar in Stockholm, Sweden. In the course of the discussion, the topic of power came up. When I mentioned surge suppressors, few people in the room knew what I was talking about, since they are not widely used in Sweden.

"LET ME GUESS - NO SURGE PROTECTORS...RIGHT?"

The surge suppressors described above simply add components in parallel with the circuit. More expensive surge suppressors use a series design, with components placed between the equipment and the AC power line. This design can provide faster *clamping*, or response to surges, than non-series designs. Due to several factors, including cost, size and heat dissipation, most surge supressors using a series design also include shunt devices.

Some surge suppressors provide for common mode suppression. Most, however, ignore common mode problems. In fact, because most surge suppressors shunt surges to neutral or ground, common mode defects can actually be increased. The best surge suppressors provide a balanced circuit, preventing a large difference in voltage or current between any of the three power circuit conductors (hot, neutral and ground).

There is some controversy over the necessity of using surge protectors with PCs. There is a faction in the industry that says surge suppressors, without a considerable amount of filtering, will not eliminate problems associated with "fast-edged" power defects. Using the bullet versus baseball analogy (see *Defect Size versus Defect Speed* above), there may be some truth to this viewpoint. The *Personal System/2 Installation Planning* manual from IBM (February, 1992) states:

> *External surge suppressors are not required on IBM PC and PS/2 systems. These systems have been designed to meet the IBM corporate requirements that include levels considered adequate for product protection.*
>
> *External surge suppression equipment have been known to be the source of difficult to diagnose system problems. No design or performance standards have been established. There is no easy way to test them.*

In addition, the Federal Information Processing Standards (FIPS 94, September 1983) recommend against the use of surge suppressors on circuits that support computer systems.

Underwriters' Laboratories (UL) has published a specification for performance of surge protectors known as UL 1449. Although this specification does require certain levels of performance, the fine print will tell you that UL does not claim that 1449 performance levels will be adequate for your needs.

As noted earlier, there is no good way to test a surge protector in the field that will not destroy it in the process. The question of whether surge protectors merely move power defects from one part of the power distribution system to another is still a matter of debate, and also seems to depend somewhat on surge protector design. In addition to surge protection, some surge protectors do provide EMI/RFI filtering (described below), and, depending on design, they may provide common mode protection, something usually not handled by PC power supplies (of course, the debate still rages as to its necessity). In any case, you may want to select them with care, or investigate transformer-based line conditioners (described below).

Under-Voltage versus Over-Voltage. A number of studies[6] have indicated that more data loss and equipment damage is caused by under-voltage conditions than by over-voltage conditions. Surge protectors do not protect against under-voltage conditions.

Power Line Filters. Power line filters remove extraneous low-voltage impulses and noise. Some surge suppressors provide some level of filtering, most commonly EMI/RFI filtering. At the high end are products that provide input filtering, surge suppression, output filtering and sine tracking (filtering noise in relation to the sine wave of the power signal). Many of these units are, in effect, hybrids, combining the features of surge protectors and power line filters. In truth, the line between high-end surge suppressors and high-end power line filters will probably blur eventually. Unfortunately, high-quality power line filters are significantly more expensive than surge suppressors.

---

[6]One such study, titled "*Effects of Power Line Disturbances on Electronic Products*," by Kenneth B. Bowes, was published in the October, 1990 issue of *Power Quality* magazine.

Power Conditioners. Power conditioners use transformers and other components to isolate electronic equipment from the power lines to effectively eliminate most power quality problems. Proponents of power conditioners contend that they are the only effective defense against many of the fast-edged power disturbances that affect computers and other high-speed electronic equipment. Some power conditioners use low-impedance transformers and some use high-impedance ferro-resonant transformers (See *High or Low Impedance Output* above). Unfortunately, power conditioners are usually significantly more expensive than surge suppressors and power line filters, usually retailing for more than $200.

Lightning Arrestors. Lightning tends to affect equipment in rural areas more than in urban areas, primarily because rural power lines tend to be more exposed to lightning than urban power lines. Since lightning is one "power defect" that is definitely known to damage equipment, it is something that you probably want to protect against. Proper grounding is the first step in lightning protection and will greatly reduce the chance of equipment damage. An inexpensive lightning arrestor, properly installed at the service entrance to the building, will reduce the chance of damage even further.

Voltage Regulating Transformers. Voltage regulating transformers maintain a constant voltage to the equipment. They are generally designed to accept power input between approximately 100 and 130 volts and provide a constant 120 volt output. PC power supplies do not require regulation in this range; therefore, voltage regulating transformers are redundant at best.

Protection for Telephone Connections. Telephone and data communications lines are susceptible to a number of types of interference, most commonly lightning-induced surges and *sneak current* (continuous extraneous current caused by miswiring and other factors). Sneak current can destroy modems and computers. With some LAN cards and cabling systems, primarily those that use coaxial cable, surges induced in one computer on a LAN can travel through the LAN and damage other equipment. A number of companies, including ONEAC, Cylix Corporation and The Siemon Company, provide protection devices that can be installed in the wiring closet or at the equipment location. According to some experts, to be effective, protection for communications equipment must be installed as near to the equipment being protected as possible.

Protection for LAN Connections. At least two companies, Cylix Corporation and Panamax, supply surge suppressors for LAN connections. Power protection devices on LAN cables do have the potential to degrade high-frequency LAN signals. Since modern, twisted-pair cabling systems provide a high degree of electrical isolation, there is some dispute as to the need for such protection in a properly designed and installed LAN.

Building-to-Building LAN Connections. If possible, LAN connections between buildings should use fiber optic or other non-copper links (such as infrared or laser beam) between buildings to provide electrical isolation and prevent ground loops. This is especially true if the connection is being run above ground, with cable suspended between buildings or on poles. Suspended cabling is obviously much more susceptible to the effects of lightning than cable run underground.

Electrostatic Discharge. Some of the highest voltage surges that your equipment may be subjected to are caused by electrostatic discharge, commonly called *static*. Static is most common in low-humidity climates, but it occurs everywhere. Static discharges are often in the range of thousands of volts, and continuous static discharge can have a cumulative effect on semiconductors (computer chips are made up of semiconductors). Small, unseen static discharges can be responsible for numerous problems that appear to be memory- or CPU-related. Our ability to detect or feel static discharges starts somewhere around 3,000 to 6,000 volts. Unfortunately, most semiconductors will fail at 3,000 volts or less. There are several methods available to combat static, including touch pads, wrist straps, anti-static equipment mats and anti-static spray. Probably the best approaches, however, are low-static carpet, humidifiers, and anti-static chair mats. If you use anti-static chair mats, you should be aware that caster-mounted chairs (in other words, most office chairs) and insulated shoes can defeat the ability of anti-static chair mats to control static. You should also be aware that standard plastic chair mats can actually increase a static problem. The clothes people wear can also contribute to static problems, building static charges as they sit in their chairs, so you might consider banning cheap polyester suits! Barring that, consider using anti-static spray on office chairs on a regular basis.

Preventing and Resolving Power Problems

Unfortunately, with so little independent information available concerning power problems and solutions, it is difficult for LAN designers, installers and managers to make sound decisions about power protection. In order to minimize the effect of power problems, follow the guidelines outlined in this chapter concerning your electrical and LAN cabling systems. You should also do your best to make a determination as to the types of power protection devices needed in your system and install them, and don't forget protection on the phone lines. You might want to employ the assistance of a qualified electrical engineer.

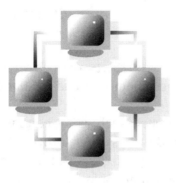

8

Business Resumption Planning

*T*here are numerous potential disasters that can destroy your office or make it otherwise unavailable. Among the possibilities:

- A fire destroys your building or office.

- An office on a floor above yours burns, and your office is flooded by the runoff from the fire hoses.

- A transformer explodes in the basement, contaminating the building with PCBs. It will be weeks, months or even years before anyone is allowed to enter.

- A construction crane falls from the roof of a building across the street, damaging your building. For safety reasons your building is evacuated until the crane is removed and the damage is repaired.

■   A natural disaster, such as an earthquake, hurricane or flood, damages or destroys your office. In this type of regional disaster, even if your office survives, critical services, such as power and telephone, may be unavailable for weeks or months after.

■   A fire in a telephone switching office takes out voice and data communications in your area for an extended period of time.

All of the above have one thing in common: they have all happened. There is little you can do to prevent these types of disasters—the best you can do is be prepared for them. You may also notice that some of the disasters listed, such as a crane falling from another building, are not things for which you would specifically plan. This means that you need to be prepared for anything that will make your business site unavailable or unusable for a short or long period of time.

As LAN-based systems become more "mission-critical," the need for off-site recovery in case of disaster increases. Unfortunately, because of the diverse nature of LAN-based systems, it is difficult to apply a "cookie-cutter" approach to recovery sites. Each organization's business resumption plan will probably have to be unique.

Simplifying the Problem

Picture this:

Your business facility is gone. It has been destroyed by fire, hurricane or some other disaster, natural or man-made. All of the information that you need to continue or resume business is stored on one or more magnetic tapes that you wisely had stored in a secure, off-site facility.

What do you do now? If you haven't planned for this eventuality, your business may not survive.

Approaches to Off-Site Recovery

There are at least five basic approaches you can take to off-site business recovery:

- Maintain a permanent recovery site.

- Use another office of your own company as a recovery site.

- Establish a "mutual aid pact" with another company to provide each other facilities in case of emergency.

- Plan to use a commercial recovery site.

- Plan to use rented space and acquire equipment when and as needed.

All of these approaches have advantages and disadvantages.

Permanent Recovery Site

Creating your own permanent recovery site has the advantage of giving you absolute control over the facility. It does, however, have several disadvantages:

- It is costly to maintain. Most organizations would have a difficult time justifying both the initial costs and ongoing maintenance expenditures required for such a facility.

- It is difficult to keep equipment up to date. Personal computers and applications are evolving at a rapid rate. It is getting more and more difficult to run new applications on old equipment. You may need to replace equipment every couple of years.

- It requires staffing. Someone will have to test and maintain the equipment.

- You need to be careful choosing the site to make sure it is available and accessible in the event of a regional disaster.

To Be Successful with this Approach: You should follow the general guidelines outlined later in this chapter, and you should constantly monitor your hardware, space and voice and data communications needs. If you use this approach, you should devise a method to send copies of your backup tapes to this site, as well as your regular off-site storage location, at least daily. This approach probably works best for systems that are centrally administered or for specific groups within an organization.

Another Office of Your Company

Using another office of your own company, assuming you have more than one office, is also an option. Advantages of this approach include:

- If properly planned, there is little extra capital investment or maintenance cost.

- If both offices have similar systems, use substantially the same software and use consistent setups, recovery time can be kept to a minimum because that office's staff will be familiar with your system.

- By working in shifts, costs can be kept down during the recovery period.

There are, however, disadvantages:

■   Working in shifts is difficult at best. The inconvenience for all concerned may translate into lost productivity, thus offsetting any cost savings. In most cases, you should consider this a short-term option.

■   You need to make sure the site is available and accessible in the event of a regional disaster.

To Be Successful with this Approach: You should follow the guidelines outlined under *Permanent Recovery Site* above. Consider the fact that an office used by one group will now be shared by two. It is very easy to exceed capacity in this situation. Constant monitoring of your growth is required.

Mutual Aid Pact

A mutual aid pact with another company is similar to using another office of your company as a recovery site. It has all the disadvantages of that approach, plus a couple of others:

■   Security may be an issue. Your business information may be more accessible to the other company's personnel than you would like.

■   It is very easy to overstay your welcome. (This works both ways.) Consider this a *very* short-term approach.

To Be Successful with this Approach: Follow the guidelines under *Another Office of Your Company* above. Be very careful about overstaying your welcome.

Commercial Recovery Site

A number of companies that provide mainframe recovery sites are now providing recovery sites for LANs. The advantage of this approach is that the recovery company's staff takes care of all maintenance. There are, however, some disadvantages:

■ Commercial recovery sites are costly. The cost, however, may be somewhat offset by savings in insurance premiums. This may also be true of other recovery options.

■ You may need to fit a rather narrow profile. Recovery site configurations tend to be pretty generic. If you have very specialized needs, this approach may not work for you.

■ Commercial recovery sites are usually available on a first-come, first-served basis. In the event of a regional disaster this could be a problem.

To Be Successful with this Approach: To be successful with this approach, you should follow the guidelines outlined under *Permanent Recovery Site* above. Because these sites are usually first-come, first-served, have *Plan B* ready.

Equipment Acquisition Plan

A fifth approach is to plan to rent space and acquire equipment when and as needed. At first glance, this appears to be the riskiest of the approaches outlined here. It does, however, offer some real benefits:

■ There is no major capital investment in advance, nor are there any ongoing monthly costs until a disaster occurs.

■ Equipment is not sitting unused, becoming obsolete.

- This approach offers a lot of flexibility for recovery site location.

- This approach can accommodate the fast-paced changes of LANs more readily than other approaches.

Among the disadvantages:

- With an established, already-set-up facility, you can often be up and running in a few hours. This approach, however, will require a day or two, and possibly more, to get going.

- Without a well-thought-out acquisition plan, vital equipment may not be available when needed.

- You may need to accept equipment that is not your first choice. When you are obtaining equipment in a hurry, you can't always afford to be choosy about brands.

- More coordination is required to get the recovery team to the proper site.

To Be Successful with this Approach: You need to have locations selected in advance. These could be hotel facilities or vacant buildings. You should also have more than one potential site selected. If your LAN uses easily available, off-the-shelf components, your emergency acquisition will be easier. In a regional disaster a local vendor may not be able to help you. Consider using vendors with a national presence, who can ship from and to multiple locations. You should have purchase agreements with more than one vendor, as well as open purchase orders. Be prepared to pay a premium for immediate delivery, and make sure your vendors are willing and able to ship when required. Consider keeping spares of critical equipment, such as a tape backup unit and software, stored in a location away from your office so it can be shipped to the recovery site by air in case of emergency. Do the same with recovery documentation. Plan in advance for communications lines, both voice and data. Check with the phone companies and data communications carriers at your proposed recovery sites in advance so you know what will be required to make installation go smoothly and quickly. Have a plan for contacting the members of the recovery team, as well as the rest of your staff, to advise them of your chosen location, and make sure they can get there.

Recovery Planning Tips

Here are some tips for recovery planning:

- Recovery time is the key issue. Make sure that your plan will allow you to recover in the allotted time.

- For a recovery plan to be successful, it requires cooperation from and coordination with all concerned, including users, department managers and top management.

- A written plan is mandatory. Steps will be forgotten if they are not written down.

- In a large organization, you may want to have different plans for different groups or departments. In this case, the central IS group can act as a coordinator and facilitator, making sure that plans are properly written. In the event of emergency, IS can provide assistance where and when needed.

- Periodic testing of the plan, as well as all software, hardware and procedures, is critical. If you do not have a permanent site, complete testing may be difficult. In this case, test as many components of the plan as possible.

■ Recovery sites should be located somewhere that will not be affected by a regional disaster, such as a hurricane, earthquake or flood.

■ When writing your plan, assume that no systems personnel will be available. All recovery instructions should be usable by nontechnical people. Document even the most basic items, such as how to put a tape in the tape drive.

■ Detailed, specific setup instructions must be part of the recovery documentation. This should include basics, such as how to install cables, how to recover data from backup tapes and how to turn on servers and workstations

■ If security information is not restored properly or overwritten, you may not be able to access system resources. Make sure your recovery documentation covers how to access needed resources when specific individuals are not available. Have a written, tested plan in place for maintaining or restoring security.

■ If you have equipment that needs to be set up at a recovery site, make sure all equipment and connectors are labeled so that setup can be accomplished by someone unfamiliar with the equipment.

■ If you have a permanent site, plan and test any required remote communications links on a regular basis. If you will be setting up a recovery site on an ad-hoc basis, make sure you keep up to date on the communications carriers' policies and procedures for emergency lines. Also, be aware that telephone companies and other communications carriers change their offerings periodically. Keep up to date on possible new offerings that provide better service, quicker installation or more flexibility.

■ Your recovery site must be accessible by your recovery team. This usually means, among other things, that the site should be accessible by car (airports can be closed) without crossing bridges. Note that freeways are often closed during emergencies, so plan for alternate routes.

■ When building your plan start from possible local disasters, then move toward regional ones. You may want to write different plans for different type of disasters. For example, if only your office building is affected, you may want to plan on a nearby recovery site. In a regional disaster, however, you probably need to consider a site a considerable number of miles away to make sure the recovery site is not affected by the same disaster.

■ Determine at which point recovery doesn't matter. Planning for recovery from total thermonuclear war, for example, may not make a lot of sense for most organizations. (Unless, of course, you plan to rule over what's left of the world!)

■ To the best of your ability, determine critical functions, the required number and types of users, files, applications and communications links. The problem with this type of planning, however, is that certain assumptions must be made about what or who is critical. Unfortunately, relative importance of resources in a LAN environment can change from day to day. This part of a plan should be a guideline and should not preclude the ability to access resources not on your list. For example, even if your plan says that certain types of data or files are not critical, plan to have them available anyway.

■ When planning for personnel availability, plan for job functions, not specific individuals. In times of crisis, specific individuals may not be available. This means that cross-training is very important so that more than one or two people can do each job or task.

- Build short-term and long-term plans. A disaster that allows you to return to your office in a few days will have a different impact than one that keeps you away for months. A disaster that destroys a building will have a different impact than one that makes it temporarily unavailable.

- Plan for local and regional disasters. A disaster that affects only your building or office can be handled differently than one that affects an entire city or geographic area.

- Effective planning requires constant reassessment because needs change over time. It is critical that all concerned be involved in the planning and reassessment processes.

- Keep important documents, such as recovery manuals and employee address and phone number lists, in the possession of every member of the recovery team and at the recovery or off-site storage site, and keep them up to date.

- If specific individuals are not available, how will you get access to critical data? Someone at the recovery site will need supervisor-level access to servers or hosts. If you have a permanent recovery site, keep required passwords in a locked safe there. If you do not have a permanent site, you will need to plan for a way to guarantee access to data in an emergency while still maintaining security. One method is to have your law or accounting firm keep passwords in sealed envelopes and remote offices. If you take this approach, you must make sure the passwords are up to date and that there are procedures in place for obtaining them in an emergency.

- If you are using a commercial recovery site, remember that they are usually available on a first-come, first-served basis. This means that it is a good idea to have "Plan B" ready.

■ How will you restore data when you return to your permanent office, or how will you recover from recovery? Many organizations have found that if they worked with subsets of data during an emergency, there was no easy way to reintegrate new and changed data back into the full database. If you take this approach, reintegration needs to be part of your plan.

■ What about user data stored on local hard disks? How will you restore it at a recovery site to get the user up and running quickly? By storing data and applications on servers instead of local hard disks, you can cut down on the time required to get each user up and running.

■ Use easy-to-obtain, off-the-shelf components. This can make it easier to get up and running quickly if you have to obtain new equipment. In an emergency, you can't afford to wait weeks or months for new equipment.

After the Fact: Problems Encountered by Those Who Have Been There

Learning from the mistakes of others is usually a lot less painful than learning from your own mistakes. After every major disaster, the popular press, business press and computer industry press will run articles about companies which survived or didn't survive that particular disaster. Reading this kind of story is a great way to discover holes in your own recovery plans. Here are a few examples of the kind of things some people found out during and after disasters:

■ **The disaster that was planned for was not the one that was experienced.** By planning only for the most likely disasters or specific disasters, you leave yourself exposed. It is a good idea to also plan for the effects of disasters in general. For example, in addition to planning for a fire or earthquake specifically, plan in general for your building being unavailable for use. In other words, plan for the possible effects of disaster in general in addition to specific disasters.

- **The plan was out of date.** All disaster plans are out of date the minute they are written. Writing plans that are flexible and don't try to account for every detail can help in this area. In addition, you should establish a mechanism for keeping your plans reasonably up to date.

- **Voice and data links created serious bottlenecks.** We often don't realize the importance of our links to the outside world until we don't have them. If you have learned to rely on a 1.5 Mbps T-1 data link, don't assume that a 56 Kbps link will do in emergency. Also, if you think people can share phone lines in an emergency, just try to do it under normal circumstances! Most of us rely on the telephone being available immediately. Plan for voice and data services at your recovery site that provide capabilities reasonably similar to those at your office.

- **Lack of realistic tests created surprises when the real thing happened.** A few years ago, one company went to run a disaster test on their mainframe system, something the new operations manager understood should be done on a regular basis. He had some outside consultants come in as observers. He felt that since his staff was busy implementing the plan, they could not note problems or determine how well the test went. During the test, the observers noted a whole slew of things that the operators did *that were not in the disaster plan*, but that they did because of their knowledge. In effect, the operators, who new the procedures well, were able to "fill in the holes" in the recovery documentation. Unfortunately, many of the undocumented tasks that the operators performed would not have been known to someone else who might have had to perform the recovery tasks in an emergency. Thus, for instance, if a particular individual had not been dealing with the tape systems, that function would probably have failed.

- **The test itself created a disaster.** In the above example, the test was a total failure. At one point the power to the mainframe's power backup and conditioning system was turned off (to simulate a real power outage), and the mainframe went down. It turned out that the CPU was not plugged into the backup system. Then the backup generator did not kick in, which was actually luck since the power line supplying the mainframe was unconditioned! Needless to say, the result was costly, and several people lost their jobs.

- **The emergency equipment acquisition plan did not work.** An acquisition plan is only as good as the vendors' ability to deliver. In a regional disaster, for example, a local vendor may also be affected and may not be able to deliver products. If you have not made arrangements in advance, or your needs are too specific, even national vendors may not be able to help. Negotiating standing purchase orders with more than one vendor and using easily available components can help.

- **The planned-for, acceptable downtime had changed.** As desktop computers and LANs become more critical to an organization's operation, the amount of downtime that is acceptable will diminish. Constant reassessment can help in this area.

- **The needed personnel were not available.** In 1992, Hurricane Andrew leveled much of South Florida. A number of businesses that survived relatively unscathed still had major problems, however, because critical staff members were unable or unwilling to come to work. Many people whose homes were destroyed or damaged were more concerned, and rightly so, about taking care of their families than they were about their jobs.

Many planners assume that their staff members will be available in an emergency. While there are numerous stories of people heroically going to great degrees of effort and hardship above and beyond the call of duty in disasters, assuming that this is automatic can be disastrous. Most LAN support people do not view themselves as soldiers or marines who must risk their lives and their families for the company. If you need to rely on your personnel being available, your plans should address the issue of caring for their families if necessary.

The "Right" Way

Unfortunately, there is too little information available about actual experiences with off-site LAN recovery to make blanket statements about what is the "right" way to do things. You need to make plans that seem to have a reasonable chance of succeeding with your circumstances and organization. In addition, the plans you design today may not work tomorrow, so you need to constantly watch for changes that could require you to reassess and rewrite portions of your plans.

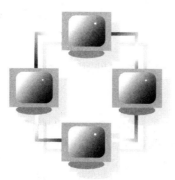

9

Writing and Testing a Recovery Plan

*T*he purpose of a disaster recovery plan is to assist in the resumption of business functions as quickly and effectively as possible after a disaster. LAN recovery plans are only a subset of that. As stated earlier, it has become nearly impossible to separate LAN recovery plans from business recovery plans as a whole. This means that your LAN recovery planning must be coordinated with the rest of the business recovery planning.

A disaster recovery plan should address the following issues:

- Reduce confusion following a disaster.

- Minimize the number of decisions that must be made following a disaster.

■ Identify the actions that must be undertaken to recover from a disaster.

■ Identify those people, or *recovery teams*, who will be responsible for implementing disaster plans, while minimizing dependence on the participation of specific individuals or groups of people during the recovery process.

■ Determine off-site locations and facilities for the storage of backup tapes, documentation, emergency equipment, forms and supplies.

■ Identify off-site business recovery sites or potential sites.

■ Plan for relocation to a business recovery site.

■ Plan for delivery of backup tapes, documentation, emergency equipment, forms and supplies from an off-site storage facility, if necessary.

■ Plan for the acquisition of required equipment, materials and services.

■ Establish priorities for critical systems or resources that must be reestablished first.

■ Provide a plan for testing the recovery plan(s) in a realistic but nondisruptive manner.

■ Provide for training and cross-training of individuals who will be involved in the recovery process.

■ Establish a notification process for those individuals who must be contacted in event of an emergency.

It is important to recognize that every disaster recovery plan is outdated the minute it is written. Therefore, a disaster plan should be considered a guide to recovery, not a substitute for thought and judgment. The members of the recovery teams must have the knowledge and ability (and the freedom) to adjust the plan as necessary during a crisis. Keeping recovery plans as up to date as possible, however, will eliminate the necessity for too many "judgment calls."

Disaster planning does not eliminate the need for good day-to-day procedures and documentation. In fact, you are much more likely to recover from a disaster if you have good documentation and procedures in place.

The Role of IS

The diverse and changing nature of LANs makes top-down, mainframe-style disaster planning at best difficult to do and at worst impossible to do. It is nearly impossible, in a large organization, for a central IS group to know with any degree of certainty which files are critical to a particular department or workgroup at any given moment. Unless you can totally control which applications are used, where all files are stored, and how every network resource is used, you will have great difficulty writing a complete, top-down recovery plan. The role of IS, however, is key to successful overall planning. A central IS group can do the following:

■ Coordinate and facilitate departmental or workgroup planning. Make sure that the plans are done and make sure all bases are covered.

■ Coordinate emergency relocation plans, emergency communications plans, emergency equipment acquisition plans, off-site storage plans and so on.

- Review plans for completeness and effectiveness. IS may not know all the issues for each department, but by reviewing plans from many departments, you can look for both strong and weak points and thereby help improve all of them.

- Provide recovery plans for company-wide resources. This could include, for example, a corporate e-mail server, customer database server or backbone network.

Phases of a Disaster Plan

An effective disaster plan should be divided into phases or steps. Although there are no hard and fast rules about how you define the steps, those outlined below should be useful, at least for initial planning. Please note that any given plan that you write may include more detailed intermediate steps. Also, some plans might be subsets of others and may not include all the steps described below.

Planning

In the planning phase, you gather information and formulate the procedures that are to be implemented in case of disaster.

Preparation

Preparation deals with those activities that need to be addressed before a disaster occurs, including off-site storage of materials, arranging for recovery sites, arranging for emergency acquisition of materials and equipment, development of priorities and training.

Testing

Your disaster plans need to be tested periodically. Tests should be scheduled on a regular basis. Tests need to be as realistic as possible without undue disruption of normal business activities. It is also a good idea to invite outside observers to participate in your tests. An outsider can often spot activities that are carried out during a test but not documented in the recovery manuals. If you are not satisfied with the results of a test, reevaluate your plan and procedures and test again as soon as possible.

Disaster Occurrence

When a disaster occurs, you may not initially have a written plan immediately available. It is important that people are knowledgeable of, trained in and practiced at initial emergency procedures, such as evacuation, shutdown of equipment and initial responses to different types of disasters.

Response

After initial emergency procedures, an assessment of the situation must be made, followed by a decision concerning the proper course of action. If your plan is well written, the number of responses will be minimized. Using a flow chart approach (described later in this chapter) can help with the decision process.

Emergency Operation

This is your mode of operation until things can return to normal. Your emergency operation mode will vary with the type of disaster and your response. It is difficult to test the long-term effectiveness of this phase of a disaster plan, so be prepared to make changes quickly.

Reconstruction/Repair

After most disasters, something will have to be rebuilt or repaired, whether it is a building, a file server, a communications link or something else. This may seem like a good opportunity for upgrades, and it may well be, but be careful. Upgrades, unless very well planned and implemented, can often increase the complexity of returning to normal operation.

Return to Normal Operation

This phase includes everything that is required to allow resumption of normal business operation. This could include moving back into permanent quarters from a recovery site or re-integrating subsets of data into a larger database. This phase requires careful planning and attention to detail to avoid creating new disasters.

Wrap-Up

In this phase, you tie up any loose ends, evaluate the results of the disaster and document any unexpected problems and new solutions encountered during and after the disaster.

Update Documentation and Training

Using what you learned, now is the time to update system documentation, if necessary, as well as modify your training programs and train people in any new procedures.

Review and Update Disaster Plan

Based on your experiences during and after the disaster, make any necessary adjustments to the plan.

Creating Scenarios

One important step in the process of disaster planning is to create likely scenarios and decide how you will respond to them. Keep this as generic as possible, such as *Loss of Facility* rather than *Fire Burns Down Building*. Listed here are a few possible scenarios, some examples, and some possible responses.

Complete Loss of Facility, Including Equipment and Supplies

The building and all contents are destroyed or otherwise made unavailable.

Examples:

■ A fire completely destroys the building.

■ A hurricane ravages the entire area, destroying billions of dollars worth of property. The U.S. has experienced several major hurricanes in recent years, including Hurricane Andrew in Florida in 1992.

■ A flood causes widespread damage and makes roads impassable. An example is the Mississippi River flood of 1993.

The most probable response here is to move to an emergency recovery site.

Facility Severely Damaged or Otherwise Unavailable, but Critical Equipment and Supplies Can Be Removed

Examples:

■ The Loma Prieta earthquake in Northern California in 1989 severely damaged many buildings. In many cases, however, equipment and supplies could be removed.

■ A fire at an AT&T telephone switching station in Hinsdale, Illinois caused no direct damage to businesses in the area, but made voice and data communications unavailable. In effect, businesses in the area had to relocate if they wanted to communicate with the rest of the world.

The most probable response in cases like this is to recover equipment and supplies and move to an emergency recovery site.

Partial Facility Damage, Requiring Relocation of One or More Departments or Workgroups

Much of the building can be occupied, but some functions need to be relocated. For example:

- A minor fire in an office, and the water damage caused by putting out the fire, make an area in an office building uninhabitable for a period of time.

- Asbestos is discovered in one section of a building during minor remodeling, forcing the relocation of staff during removal.

There are two probable responses to this kind of situation. Move affected equipment and personnel into other areas of the building or to a recovery site.

We Are All at Risk

In case you think you're in a safe building or an area not affected by natural disasters, note the following:

- In 1992, a hole was accidentally punched into a wall holding back water from the Chicago River, flooding the basements of many downtown office buildings. Most of the buildings' power and communications distribution systems were in the basements. In addition, several data centers were also located in basements.

- In 1993, a terrorist bomb exploded in the underground parking garage of the World Trade Center in New York. Businesses located in the center were displaced for months.

In both these instances, it would have been highly unlikely that anyone would have planned for the specific disaster. By planning for the effects, no matter how unlikely the cause, your plan can cover you.

Flow Charts

Flow charts can help you determine if the structure and logic of your plans are effective. Flow charts are also a good way to simplify the decision-making process. The flow charts at the end of this chapter illustrate this. Figure 9-1 illustrates a sample disaster-planning flow chart. In this example, a major direction is chosen based on whether the disaster means that the business site is unavailable. In this case, two possible courses of action are indicated: move to a recovery site, or implement an appropriate emergency procedure.

Figure 9-2 illustrates an off-site recovery plan. Again, the number of major decisions that need to be made is limited.

Figure 9-3 illustrates one possible scenario for a disaster that does not require a recovery site. Again, with proper planning, the number of decisions that need to be made is limited.

Recovery Teams

A recovery team is a group of people charged with the task of recovering from a disaster. Just as you may have more than one plan, you may also have more than one recovery team. Different teams could be responsible for different functions or different workgroups or departments. It is important that recovery team members be:

■   Knowledgeable of and practiced in the tasks that they will be required to perform.

■ Available in the event of disaster. This could be a major concern in the event of a regional disaster, where family considerations might come first, or damage to roads or bridges could prevent access.

■ Cross-trained. Because you cannot be sure who will be available in a disaster, team members not only need to know how to handle the tasks of other members of their own team, but, if you have multiple teams, should be able to handle the tasks of members of other teams as well. Good documentation, as well as consistency between different systems, can be a big help here.

You might also want to arrange for backup recovery personnel. Making contingency plans in advance with your LAN reseller is one approach. Maintaining good relations, especially with their support people, can go a long way in making sure this approach is successful.

Communicating with Team Members

If disaster strikes, how will you contact recovery team members? What if someone is unavailable? You need to make sure up-to-date phone lists are in the hands of all members of the recovery team. You should also have a plan for notifying team members who are away from home.

In the event of a regional disaster, telephone service, if available at all, will be difficult to use because circuits will constantly be busy. How will you contact your team? You may want to prearrange a plan to meet at your business site, if it is accessible, or at a recovery site if it is not.

Travel Arrangements

How will your recovery team(s) get to your recovery site? What if a regional disaster takes out bridges, roads or airports? What about lodging? Your plan needs to address these issues.

Family

In the event of a regional disaster, people will be more concerned about their families than about your LAN. One way to handle this is to use the Pony Express method—only hire unmarried orphans. If this approach isn't practical, you should consider what will need to be done to make sure your staff can put their attention on disaster recovery for your system. There are no easy answers to this problem, and very few disaster plans even address the issue.

Communications

How will you restore communications with the outside world after a disaster, especially if you have moved to a different site? If you have not planned in advance, you may be in for some surprises. Also, lack of communications may force you to move to a recovery site. A few years ago, a fire in a telephone switching station knocked out phone service to the surrounding area for weeks, putting some companies out of business.

Here are a few things about communications to keep in mind:

- Arrange for communications services for your recovery site in advance, and make sure those arrangements are well documented, including contact names. This information should be included with the recovery team name and address lists that are in the possession of each team member, and should also be stored at the recovery site and/or the off-site storage location.

- Among the criteria for selecting a recovery site should be the ability to quickly implement the communications services that you need.

- Never assume that you can get by with substantially less communications capability during an emergency. In fact, you will probably find both voice and data communications to be more essential during an emergency than they are when the business is running normally.

- How easily and quickly can you replace critical communications components, such as routers or DSU/CSUs (Digital Service Unit/Communications Service Units)? This should be part of your selection criteria for these products.

Required Equipment and Supplies

What equipment will you need at your recovery site? What supplies? Your plan should list:

- Equipment and supplies that you know that you will need. Because LAN systems change so rapidly, you will not be able to list everything. Using easily available, off-the-shelf equipment, however, will make emergency acquisition easier.

- Location of backup inventories, and how to access those inventories. Backup inventories should include copies of any software required to restore data and bring up new workstations and servers. Avoid storing supplies that can be easily obtained, such as standard office furniture, printer paper and toner.

- Vendors that have been contracted to supply equipment or other material in an emergency. Locations, contact names, phone numbers and contract information, including any standing purchase order information, should be included. You should have more than one vendor for each product type, and those vendors should be able to get products to your recovery site quickly.

Equipment Inventory

A comprehensive listing of existing hardware and software is essential for determining what will be needed in an emergency. It is also important for ensuring that insurance coverage is adequate and for proof-of-loss after a disaster. A copy of the inventory should be stored at the recovery site or off-site storage location. Maintaining such an inventory should be part of your accounting procedures or standard operating procedures.

Vendors

A list of vendors of hardware, software, services and supplies should be stored at the recovery site or off-site storage location. This list should be as comprehensive as possible, since you may not know exactly what you will need or who will be able to supply it until after disaster strikes. The list should include the vendor's name and address, telephone and fax numbers, contact names, products/services purchased, products/services supplied, and any other information that you deem important.

Important Records

In addition to those items already mentioned, up-to-date copies of the following should be stored at the recovery site or off-site-storage location:

- Master copies of software

- Accounting and corporate database records, stored both electronically and on paper

- Recovery procedure manuals

- Documentation, operation manuals and technical manuals

- Backup tapes

- Any files needed to recreate data or speed the process of disaster recovery

It should be noted that it is very important that the off-site storage location be physically secure, and that temperature and humidity be maintained within the range required for storing magnetic media.

Tools for Writing Disaster Plans

There are two basic approaches that you can take to writing your disaster plan—use specialized software or use generic software. There are a number of packages available to assist you in writing your disaster plan, and it is definitely a good idea to investigate them.[1] You may find that, in general, these packages are somewhat expensive ($4,000-50,000 or more), and they usually have a long learning curve and require training. In addition, you may also find that you have to redesign your system or procedures to use these tools effectively.

The other approach is to use the tools that you already have or, at least, more generic software. The text of a disaster plan can be created in any word processor. Information about recovery team members, vendors, inventory and so on can be extracted from other corporate applications and moved into a word processor, spreadsheet or database. Simple graphics packages, like Shapeware's VISIO, are ideal for creating flow charts.

---

[1]A number of disaster planning software packages are listed in the *Disaster Recovery Yellow Pages*, which is listed in Appendix F.)

The key here is to make sure that the approach you take allows everyone involved to maintain your disaster plans in an easy and cost-effective fashion.

Testing

Unfortunately, it is next to impossible to conduct a truly realistic test that will not significantly disrupt the operation of the organization. You can, however, conduct tests that can give you a reasonably good idea of what you can expect under certain, specific circumstances. For your tests to be meaningful, you should follow the following guidelines:

- Establish measureable objectives. What are you trying to accomplish with a test? If you cannot measure the result, you cannot determine if you have a sucessful test. For example, "Determine if we can recover from a disaster" is not a measurable objective unless you create an actual disaster. Even then, you will only know if you can recover from the specific disaster that you created, under specific circumstances. The following is a measurable objective:

  At our business recovery site, determine if we can effectively bring up a new file server, restore data from off-site tapes, bring up 10 workstations and run three major applications within 24 hours.

  In this case, there would probably be a number of secondary or supporting objectives, such as "Determine if we can install our backup software on the recovery site server and restore data."

- You must have well-documented, step-by-step procedures. If you don't, you can never be sure if you're testing your

procedures or someone's knowledge of the task at hand. You
want to make sure that you are testing your procedures.

- Keep your tests simple. Yes, during an actual emergency, things
  can get complicated. When you overcomplicate things during a
  test, however, you make it difficult to determine what went right
  and what went wrong. In addition, if problems arise, added
  complexity makes it difficult to determine the causes of those
  problems.

- If you are testing a complex procedure, break it down into
  component parts and test each part separately. If you find a
  problem in an early stage of a procedure, you can change that
  step before proceeding. This can help to prevent you from
  making false assumptions about the results of a test.

- Record the results while you are running the test. If you wait
  until later, important details will be forgotten.

- Use observers. Invite interested people who are not directly
  involved to observe. This has several benefits:

  - Someone who does not know your procedures can often
    notice if you are performing tasks that are not documented
    but should be.

  - You will help them in the development and refinement of
    their own plans.

  - Someone viewing things from a perspective different from
    your own can often see ways to solve problems that you
    might not see.

- Include people who may be involved in disaster recovery but
  may not have been involved in writing recovery procedures. As

with observers, you will probably find that you will benefit from differences in perspective. In addition, you may find that what seems obvious to you and your immediate staff may not be so obvious to other team members.

At the end of this chapter are abbreviated examples of a test procedure and a test procedure worksheet.

Conclusion

Testing is an on-going process. It is not only a way to find out if your recovery procedures work, but also a way to improve those procedures, as well as familiarize your staff with new or modified procedures. Testing should include more than your major disaster recovery procedures; it should also cover your emergency repair procedures, such as file server swaps or cable testing. Finally, if you approach testing as a training tool (and one of the best ones, at that), it will seem more like a valuable tool and less like a waste of time.

Figure 9-1: Sample Disaster Planning Flow Chart

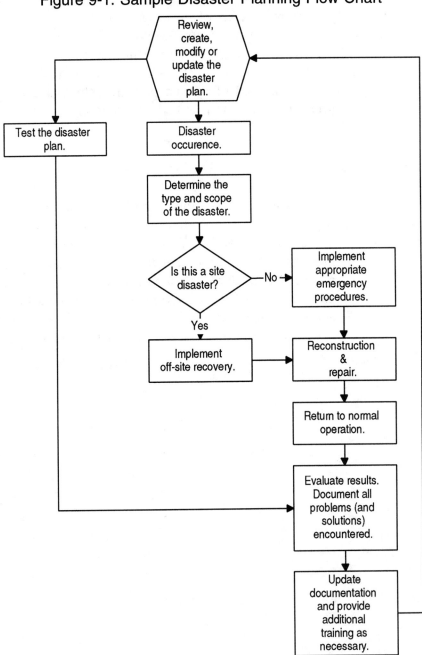

Figure 9-2: Sample Flow Chart for Site Disaster

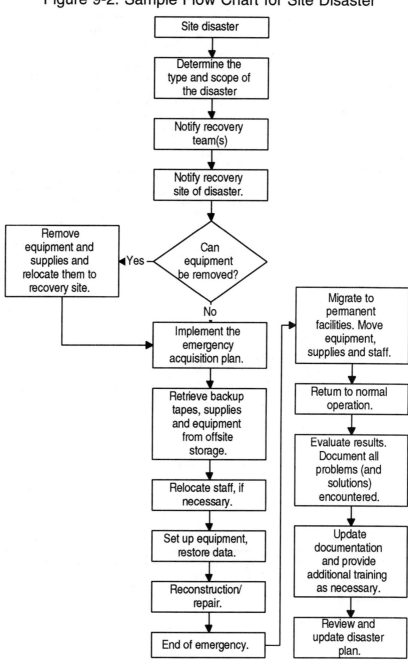

Figure 9-3: Sample Flow Chart for Server Down

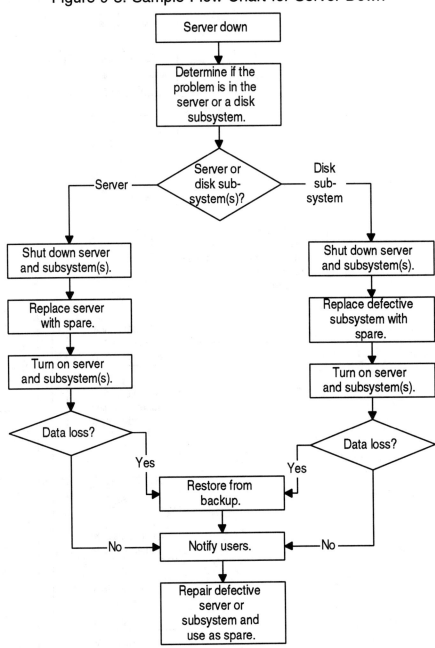

Figure 9-4: Sample Recovery Plan Test Procedures

Disaster Recovery Test Procedures

Test: Test Date:
Test Objectives:

Prior test in series:
Next test in series:

1. **Turn on file server, disk subsystems and tape drive to ensure proper operation.**
   a. Make sure that the disk drive subsystem cables are plugged into the correct file server host adapters. Ports on the server and the subsystems are labeled "A" and "B."
   b. Make sure the network cable is plugged into the file server and the hub.
   c.. Make sure that all power cords are plugged in.
   d. Turn on switches on the file server, monitor and disk subsystems.
   e. The file server should boot automatically and, after initialization, display the MONITOR screen.

2. **Load the backup software and make sure it recognizes the tape drive.**
   a. At the file server console, press <Alt><Esc> until the console's colon (:) prompt is displayed.
   b. At the prompt, type "BKSTART <Enter>" to load the backup software.
   c. From the backup software menu, highlight "Device Management" and press <Enter>.
   d. The tape drive should be displayed in the device list.

3. (next step)

4. (next step)

Figure 9-5: Sample Disaster Recovery Test Worksheet

Disaster Recovery Test Worksheet

Test: Test Date:
Test Objectives:

Prior test in series: Test Date:
Next test in series: Projected Test Date:
Participants:
Observers:

	Procedure Step	Expected Result	Acceptable Variance	Actual Result	Corrective Action
1	Turn on file server, disk subsystems and tape drive.	File server boots, recognizes hard drives and loads network operating system.	None		
2	At the file server console, load the backup software and make sure it recognizes the tape drive.	Tape drive recognized by backup software.	None		
3	(next step)				
4	(next step)				

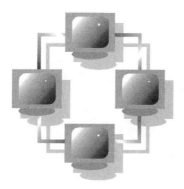

Glossary

10BASE2

IEEE 802.3 standard for thin coaxial Ethernet. 10 Mbps over baseband at up to 185 meters.

10BASE5

IEEE 802.3 standard for thick coaxial Ethernet. 10 Mbps over baseband at up to 500 meters.

10BASE-T

IEEE 802.3 standard for twisted pair Ethernet. 10 Mbps over baseband using unshielded, twisted-pair cable.

8 millimeter (8 mm)

A helical scan recording system designed by Sony for video recording that has been adapted for backup and archiving.

ampere (amp)

A measure of electrical power.

ANSI

American National Standards Institute. ANSI develops and publishes technical standards.

ANSI/EIA/TIA 568

A commercial building wiring standard originally published by the Electronic Industries Association and the Telecommunications Industries Association, then sanctioned by the American National Standards Institute.

application server

A server that is used for a specific application or applications, such as backup or archiving.

ARCNET

A widely used LAN architecture, developed by Datapoint Corporation, that uses a logical token-passing access method at 2.5 Mbps.

backup

A copy of a file, directory or volume on another storage device for the purpose of retrieval in case the original is accidentally erased, damaged or destroyed.

backup power supply (BPS)

A device that provides emergency power during power outages.

BBS

Electronic bulletin-board service.

bit

A binary digit; must be either a zero (on) or a one (off).

bit interleaving

Data is written to disk a single bit at a time, with each bit written sequentially to the next drive.

blackout

A complete loss of electrical power.

block

A unit of disk storage. DOS disks usually store data in 2 KB blocks, and Novell NetWare stores data in 4 KB blocks.

block interleaving

Data is written to disk a block at a time, with each block written sequentially to the next drive.

bridge

A device used to connect LANs by forwarding packets addressed to other similar networks across connections at the media access control sub-layer of the data link layer of the OSI model. Routers, which operate at the network layer, are sometimes erroneously called bridges.

brownout

A condition in which electrical power dips below normal for more than a few seconds. Persistent brownouts can cause data corruption and loss and can also cause computer power supplies to overheat and burn out.

Btrieve

A file manager used by many application programs. Btrieve stores and retrieves data using a B-tree access method. Btrieve is now owned by Novell and is the basis for NetWare SQL and some NetWare system functions.

bus

A common connection. Networks that broadcast signals to all stations, such as Ethernet or ARCNET, are considered bus networks.

CD-ROM

Compact disk - read-only memory. CD-ROM uses the same compact disks used for audio. CD-ROM is becoming increasingly popular as a method to distribute software and disseminate large amounts of data inexpensively. A CD-ROM disk can hold approximately 550 to 600 MB of data. CD-ROM disks, like records, are pressed, making mass production very inexpensive.

CompuServe Information Service

A commercial, on-line information service. Numerous hardware and software companies provide technical support information via CompuServe. In addition, CompuServe support forums allow users to exchange information with each other. CompuServe users can exchange electronic mail with most other public e-mail systems.

concentrator

A 10BASE-T hub. A multi-port repeater for Ethernet/802.3 over unshielded twisted-pair wire.

DAT

Digital Audio Tape. A helical scan recording system designed for audio recording that has been adapted for backup and archiving.

data striping

The process of sequentially writing data across multiple disk drives.

database server

The "back end" processor that manages the database and fulfills database requests in a client/server database system.

de facto standard

A standard based on broad usage and support.

de jure standard

An official standard developed or approved by one of the industry standard committees, such as IEEE and ANSI.

differential backup

Backing up all files that have changed since the last full backup. This approach means that no more than two sets of backup media are required for a full restore.

digital audio tape

See *DAT*.

Digital Data Storage (DDS)

The most commonly used data format for digital audio tape (DAT). A competing format, DataDAT, has virtually disappeared, leaving DDS as the de facto standard. A newer, higher-capacity format, DDS-II, is gradually replacing DDS.

disk channel

All of the components that connect disk drives to a computer, including the disk drives themselves. This includes the host adapter or disk controller and cables. See *disk duplexing*.

disk duplexing

A method of safeguarding data in which the same data is copied simultaneously to two hard disks on separate channels. If one channel fails, the data on the other channel remains unharmed. When data is duplexed, read requests are sent to whichever disk in the pair can respond faster, thus increasing the file server's efficiency. When two or more read requests occur together, the requests are split and can be processed at once. See *disk mirroring*.

disk mirroring

A method of safeguarding data in which the same data is copied to two hard disks on the same channel. If one of the disks fails, the data on the other disk is safe. Since the two disks are on the same channel, mirroring provides only limited data protection; a failure anywhere along the channel could shut down both disks and data would be lost. Also see *disk duplexing*.

dongle

A device which attaches to a computer's printer port containing a unique code that can be read by software. Dongles are used for security or software protection.

download

Copy a file from a remote computer system.

downsize

Migrate from larger computer systems to smaller ones, or reduce the size (including staff) of an organization.

downtime

Unavailability of a computer system or service.

drive spanning

The process of writing data across multiple disk drives.

dropout

An area on a disk or tape that cannot effectively record data.

duplexing

See *disk duplexing*.

e-mail

Electronic mail exchanged via computers.

encryption

The process of scrambling data so that it cannot be read by unauthorized people.

Ethernet, 802.3

The IEEE 802.3 official standard. A popular LAN architecture that uses a bus topology and CSMA/CD at 10 Mbps. Although 802.3 is technically not Ethernet, the name is commonly used because of the roots of 802.3. See *Ethernet, E.SPEC VER.1, E.SPEC VER.2*.

Ethernet, E.SPEC VER.1, E.SPEC VER.2

A proprietary LAN developed by DEC, Intel and Xerox that was the basis for the IEEE 802.3 specification. The VER.1 spec was released in September 1980, VER.2 in November 1982 and 802.3 in January 1985.

file server

A computer that provides network stations with controlled access to files and other resources.

freeware

Copyrighted software provided for use at no cost.

GB

See *gigabyte*.

Gbyte

See *gigabyte*.

GFS

Grandfather, father, son. GFS is the most commonly used backup tape rotation method. GFS works as follows: backups are performed daily, weekly and monthly. Daily tapes are rotated each week, weekly tapes are rotated each month, and monthly tapes are rotated each year.

gigabyte

A unit of measure for memory or disk storage capacity; two to the thirtieth power (1,073,741,824 bytes). Often abbreviated *GB* or *Gbyte*.

grandfather, father, son

See *GFS*.

host adapter

An adapter card to attach a device to a computer's expansion bus. Most commonly attaches SCSI devices to PCs or other computers.

host gateway

A system that provides routing and protocol conversion between personal computer users on a LAN and a time-sharing computer.

Hot Fix

A feature of NetWare that, along with read-after-write verification, protects data from hard disk defects. If data cannot be written and then read back reliably from a particular block on the hard disk, Hot Fix stores the data in the redirection area (a small portion of the hard disk reserved for this purpose during installation). The location of the defective block is added to the bad block table, and the operating system will not try to store data in that block again.

hub

1) A device used on certain network topologies that splits or amplifies signals, allowing the network to be lengthened or expanded with additional workstations. The hub is the central device in a star topology.

2) A computer that receives messages from other computers, stores them and routes them to other computer destinations.

hub port

A network connection on a hub.

IEEE

The Institute of Electrical and Electronic Engineers. A group that develops and publishes many of the official LAN-related standards, including 802.3 Ethernet and 802.5 Token Ring.

IEEE 802.3 standard

IEEE standard for Ethernet-type networks.

IEEE 802.5 standard
IEEE standard for token-passing ring networks.

intelligent drive electronics
See *IDE*.

IDE
Intelligent drive electronics, also called *integrated drive electronics*. A hard disk/controller architecture that includes most of the interface electronics on the drive itself.

internet, internetwork
Two or more networks connected by bridges and/or routers, a network of networks.

Internet
The largest internetwork in the world. Successor to ARPANET, the Internet includes other large internetworks, including MILNET, NFSNET and CREN. The Internet uses the TCP/IP protocol suite and connects universities, government agencies, businesses and individuals around the world.

Internetwork Packet Exchange
See *IPX*.

interoperability
The ability of different computer systems to communicate and work together.

I/O
Input/output. The process of moving data, as in the transmitting of data from memory to disk.

IPX
Internetwork Packet Exchange. The default protocol used by Novell's NetWare for the exchange of message packets on an internetwork.

IPX passes application requests for network services to the network drivers and on to other workstations, servers or devices on the internetwork.

ISA bus

Industry Standard Architecture. The IBM AT expansion bus.

ISO

The International Standards Organization. ISO developed the milestone Open Systems Interconnection (OSI) model.

journaling

Writing database transactions to disk or tape in a continuous, streaming fashion. Journaling is used to allow restoration of a database to a specific transaction or time period.

KB

See *kilobyte*.

KB/sec

Kilobyte per second.

Kbyte

See *kilobyte*.

kilobyte

A unit of measure for memory or disk storage capacity; two to the tenth power (1,024 bytes). Often abbreviated *KB* or *Kbyte*.

MAU

1) Media access unit. Ethernet transceiver.

2) Multi-station access unit. Token ring device used to connect several stations to the ring.

media access unit
> See *MAU*.

MB
> See *megabyte*.

MB/sec
> Megabytes per second.

Mbyte
> See *megabyte*.

megabyte
> A unit of measure for memory or disk storage capacity; two to the twentieth power (1,048,576 bytes). Often abbreviated as *MB* or *Mbyte*.

megahertz
> One million cycles per second. Often abbreviated as mHz.

metal oxide varistor
> See *MOV*.

mHz
> See *megahertz*.

MIB
> Management Information Base. A collection of objects that can be accessed via a network management protocol.

MOV
> Device used in surge protectors to shunt surges to ground or neutral.

MTBF
> Mean Time Between Failures. A figure of merit for electronic equipment or systems that indicates the average duration of periods

of fault-free operation. Used in conjunctions with mean time to repair (MTTR) to derive availability figures.

multi-station access unit

See *MAU*.

NetWare

The family of network operating systems from Novell, Inc.

NetWire

Novell-sponsored support forum on CompuServe Information Service.

optical disks

Storage medium that is read from or written to by laser beams.

OS/2

Operating System/2. Operating system created by IBM and Microsoft. No longer supported by Microsoft, IBM continues its development and support.

OSI

Open Systems Interconnection. An international standardization program to facilitate communication between computers from different manufacturers. See *ISO*.

parity

A method of checking for errors in transmitted data. The transmitting end adds the bits being transmitted. If parity is set to odd, the transmitter attaches a bit if the total is even, making it odd. If parity is set to even, the transmitter attaches a bit if the total is odd, making it even. The receiving end adds all the bits, which should always be odd for odd parity and even for even parity because of the adjustments made by the transmitter to ensure the result. If the total is of the wrong type, the communications software on the receiving end detects that an error has occurred during transmission and requests that the data be retransmitted.

protocol

Rules for communicating, particularly for the format and transmission of data.

QIC

Quarter Inch Cartridge. Tape backup format designed and promoted by 3M Corporation.

Quarter Inch Cartridge

See *QIC*.

RAID

Redundant array of inexpensive disks, also called *redundant array of independent disks*. A scheme for writing data across multiple disk drives, making them appear as a single, logical drive. Depending on the particular implementation, RAID can provide increased disk capacity and/or a level of fault tolerance.

RAM

Random access memory. A dynamic data storage location in which data can be accessed in any order.

redundant array of inexpensive disks

See *RAID*.

router

Hardware and software that routes data between similar or dissimilar networks at the Network layer of the OSI model.

SCSI

Small Computer System Interface. Usually pronounced "scuzzy." An industry standard that sets guidelines for connecting peripheral devices and their controllers to a microprocessor. The SCSI defines both hardware and software standards for communication between a host computer and a peripheral.

server

A network device that provides services to client stations. Servers include file servers, disk servers and print servers.

shareware

Software marketed on a try-before-you-buy basis. Shareware software is distributed via BBSes, on-line information services and shareware distributors.

shunt devices

Power protection devices that divert power and voltage surges from one conductor in a power circuit to another.

Simple Network Management Protocol

See *SNMP*.

Small Computer Systems Interface

See *SCSI*.

SMS

Storage Management Services. The name Novell, Incorporated has given to their strategy to solve problems related to NetWare file server backup. SMS is now supported in varying degrees by many network backup system vendors.

SNMP

Simple Network Management Protocol. The network management protocol of choice for TCP/IP-based networks, now becoming standard throughout the industry. Widely implemented with 10BASE-T Ethernet.

sneak current

Stray voltage on telephone lines.

SPS

Standby power supply. A backup power system that provides power during power outages. Unlike a UPS, an SPS does not provide continuous power.

standby power supply

See *SPS*.

star topology

A LAN topology in which each workstation connects to a central device.

star-wired ring

A ring network (such as a token-passing ring) cabled through centralized hubs or connection devices to create a physical star topology. By using a star topology, individual stations and whole sections of the network can easily be removed or added.

Storage Management Services

See *SMS*.

TCP/IP

Transmission Control Protocol/Internet Protocol. A communications protocol suite for internetwork routing and reliable message delivery; originally endorsed by the U.S. Department of Defense and implemented on ARPANET. TCP/IP is the basis of the Internet, as is widely-used in local area networks.

Thin Ethernet

The common name for 10BASE2 cabling systems. See *10BASE2*.

time-sharing host

A computer system that allows access by multiple users using terminals or terminal emulation.

token

A unique combination of bits transmitted on a token-passing network, possession of which constitutes permission to transmit data across the network.

token ring, token-passing ring

A LAN design in which each station is connected to an upstream station and a down stream station. An electronic signal, the token, is passed from station to station around the ring. A station may not send a transmission to another station unless it has possession of a "free" token, a token not currently in use. Since only one token is allowed on the network, only one station may broadcast at a time. See *star-wired ring*.

Transmission Control Protocol/Internet Protocol

See *TCP/IP*.

trojan horse

A computer program that poses as another program. Common trojan horse programs are used to intercept network users' passwords by posing as login programs.

twisted-pair wire

Two wires that are wrapped around each other to reduce induction between them. Commonly used for telephone and LAN wiring.

underrun

A condition caused by data being supplied to a tape drive at less than its transfer rate. During an underrun condition, the tape stops while the drive waits for more data to become available. The tape must then be reversed to read the last block written, and then positioned to the next block to begin the write cycle again. Underrun will degrade performance and can cause excessive head and tape wear. This condition is also referred to as shoe shining, due to the back and forth motion of the tape across the heads.

uninterruptible power supply

See *UPS*.

unshielded twisted-pair

See *twisted-pair wire*.

UPS

Uninterruptible power supply. A backup power unit that provides continuous power when the normal power supply is interrupted. UPS systems rely on regular power and/or batteries to supply it while it supplies power to the protected device.

UTP

Unshielded twisted-pair wire. See *twisted-pair wire*.

virus

A computer program designed to interfere with the normal operation of a computer system.

zener diode

A shunt device used in power protection equipment. See *shunt device*.

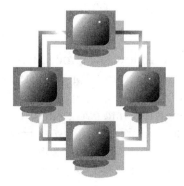

Sample Server and Workstation Recovery Plans

The following is a sample procedure for dealing with file server or workstation problems. This is not meant to be a comprehensive troubleshooting and repair guide, just an example of the type of documentation that can be helpful in an emergency.

File Server Problems

This section outlines the procedures for handling file server or server disk system problems. If a major file server problem occurs, do not attempt to repair it on line. Replace the server or affected drive subsystem with a spare, making sure you keep downtime to a minimum. Before proceeding with a repair, you must diagnose the problem. If you determine that the problem is with a file server or its components, follow the procedures below. If not, follow the appropriate repair procedures for the affected network components.

File server problems fall into two categories—internal server problems and disk subsystem problems. Internal problems mean any defective component in the server, while subsystem problems include all problems with external disk systems and cables. Server problems should be handled as follows:

1.   Internal Server Component

      a.   Power down the file server and disk systems.

      b.   Unplug cables from the file server, noting location of each cable.

      c.   Replace the file server with the spare server, then reconnect each cable in the same location. Make sure the drive cables are connected to the proper host adapters. Adapter 0 is in the second slot from the power supply, and adapter 1 is in the third slot. Each drive cable and the end of each adapter is also marked with the appropriate number. Power up the file server, then power up each drive subsystem.

      d.   Our file servers use a shareware program called DELAY-.COM[1] to make it easy to break out of the startup batch file. At the "Start file server?" prompt, type "N". The DELAY.COM program will only give you five seconds to type "N" before loading SERVER.EXE. If SERVER.EXE does execute, wait until the server initialization process

---

[1]DELAY.COM is available from many bulletin boards or from CT Services, 246 Chambers Place, Nanaimo, BC Canada V9R 6H6.

ends, shut down the server with the DOWN command, then return to DOS with the EXIT command.

e.   Copy the proper SERVER.EXE file from the DOS partition backup diskette for the file server being replaced to the C:\SERVER directory on the spare server.

f.   Restart the file server from the C:\SERVER directory by typing:

```
SERVER <Enter>
```

h.   Repair the defective server and use it as the spare.

2.   External Disk System

a.   Load the INSTALL utility at the system console to determine which disk on which channel is not functioning correctly. You can identify the disk channel by the location of its host adapter and the markings on the adapter and cable. Adapter 0 is in the second slot from the power supply and adapter 1 is in the third slot. Each drive cable and the end of each adapter is also marked with the appropriate number. Individual disks are identified by their SCSI addresses. The address switch for each disk is on the back of each subsystem. Write down the mirroring information so that you can remirror the drives later. Unmirror all disks on the problem channel.

b.   Power down the drive system(s) on that channel.

c.   If there is more than one disk subsystem on each channel, determine which subsystem has the faulty disk by looking at the SCSI addresses on the switches on the back of each subsystem.

d.   Inspect all SCSI cables and power cables for damage and make sure they are properly connected. If a cable problem is detected, reconnect or replace the cable, turn on the power to the subsystem(s) on that disk channel, then go to step h.

e.   Unplug the cables from the defective disk subsystem and remove it.

f.   Locate the spare subsystem and set it next to the old one, with the backs facing out. Make sure the SCSI addresses of the new system match those of the old system.

g.   Replace the subsystem with the spare, reattach the cables, then turn on the power to the subsystem(s) on that disk channel.

h.   Using the INSTALL utility, remirror all drives on the channel. If the problem still persists, repeat the above steps.

h.   If a defective subsystem (or any component in that subsystem) is found, repair the subsystem and use it as the spare. If a defective cable is found, order a new cable as a spare.

Workstation Problems

This section outlines the procedures for handling workstation problems. If a major workstation problem occurs, do not attempt to repair it on line. Replace the workstation with a spare, making sure you keep downtime to a minimum. Before proceeding with a repair, you must diagnose the problem. If you determine that the problem is with a workstation or its components or peripherals, follow the procedures below. If not, follow the appropriate repair procedures for the affected network components.

Workstation problems fall into two categories—internal component problems and external peripheral problems. Internal problems mean any defective component in the server, while peripheral problems include all problems with external devices such as tape drives, scanners and CD-ROMs. Workstation problems should be handled as follows:

1. Internal Workstation Components

    a. If possible, back up any user files stored on the workstation hard disk. Power down the workstation and any external peripherals.

    b. Unplug cables from the workstation, noting location of each cable.

    c. Replace the workstation with an equivalent spare, reattaching all cables. If there are peripherals that require interfaces or drivers that are unique to that workstation (i.e., not included with a standard spare), determine if the user can get by without them for a day or two. If the answer is "yes," skip to step *e*. If the answer is "no," do not attach the non-standard peripherals yet, perform the basic tests outlined in step *e*, then return to step *d*.

    d. If the user requires one or more non-standard peripherals or drives immediately, find out if the user is knowledgeable enough to install them himself or herself. If the answer is "yes," offer to assist the user in the task. If the answer is "no," you need to remove the peripheral interface from the defective machine and/or add the appropriate driver to the workstation's disk and startup files.

e. Power up the workstation, reload any user files from the most recent backup (making sure not to overwrite system and startup files, including network communications software), then test the system for network access and standard application access.

f. If non-standard peripherals still need to be reenabled, plan to do so in off hours.

g. Repair the defective station, then return it to the spares inventory.

2. Standard External Peripherals

a. Replace standard peripherals, such as monitors, mice and keyboards, with equivalent spares. If the peripherals are non-standard, you will have to research the best method for handling repair or replacement.

b. Repair or replace the peripheral and return to the spares inventory.

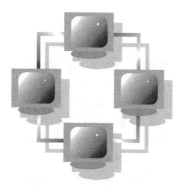

Statistics

Statistics: How Much Faith Can You Put In Them?

By Ed Devlin

The following is reprinted from the Oct./Nov./Dec. 1993 issue of *Disaster Recovery Journal*.

*H*ave you ever had a discussion where statistics became a sore point? Recently I had just such a discussion. The sore point became whether we can rely on the statistics that are presented to us. It all came about as a result of a poll taken back in May on whether President Clinton should go to the Vietnam Veterans Memorial on Memorial Day. Seventy-five percent of the people that were polled felt that the President should go to the Memorial. As the discussion grew heated, the issue became how the poll was conducted. My friend wanted to know, of the people who were polled, how many served in the Armed Forces? How many served during a War? How many were mothers whose sons or daughters were killed in a war. How many were married to people who were killed in a war? Or, the children whose parents were killed in a war? His point was that if this group of people were not represented in the poll, it could be skewed in one direction in order to present misinformation. He also wanted to know how the questions were being phrased. Were they asked if Bill Clinton should go to the Memorial, or were they asked if the President should go to the Memorial? As he explained, this information would be valuable in determining the viability of the poll.

As he became more emotional, I decided to explain that polls and statistics are used by people to support their particular position. The outcome of most polls is determined before a poll is taken. A person who wants to convince people of a specific position, will commission a group to take a sampling and create statistics that substantiate the point. If the first sample doesn't provide the desired result, they'll commission a second sampling. Remember Murphy's First Law of Statistics-"If the statistics don't support your view point, you obviously need more statistics."

I attempted to use the following example to demonstrate my point. In the Disaster Recovery/Business Resumption Planning industry there has been a statistic floating around for years that has no validity, and yet it continues to be used by people who want it to support their viewpoint. The statistic in the late 1970s was "43% of all companies that suffer a disaster in their data center go out of business within three years." Then in the early 1980s, more companies must have gone out of business because the statistic increased to "70%." A publication from Great Britain quoted it as "80%," and now in the 1990s you may see it as "90%." I guess by the year 2000, 110% of all businesses that suffer a disaster in the data center will go out of business.

You may be wondering where the statistic originated and why I say there is no validity to it. Jerry Issacson, a staff member of the Computer Security Institute, did research in December 1982 to determine the source of the statistic. The results were published in CSI's January/February 1983 newsletter.

The research traced the statistic through its many sources. The research effort found a reference in the general management publication "Boardroom Reports." They attributed the source to the insurance industry publications "Business Insurance Weekly", who in turn attributed it to a report from a seminar given by a disaster recovery consulting firm in Texas. The Texas consulting firm said they had obtained it from the National Fire Protection Association. The NFPA said they had no data to back up the figure; they don't track companies after a fire, and they have few records of computer room fires in any case. (Keep in mind that this report was written for the Jan/Feb 1983 newsletter, because the NFPA did have a story in their magazine in 1992 dealing with fires in computer centers.) The NFPA went on to say that their marketing area once published a form of that figure in a brochure, but they pointed out that it referred only to organizations that had experienced a major "industrial" fire. They subsequently withdrew it when they were unable to verify the data. CSI finally determined it came from a headline from the *Journal of Commerce*, which read: "43% of companies that had a major fire and did not have adequate business interruption insurance went out of business within 3 years." This statement appeared in the *Journal of Commerce* in 1949, one year before the first commercial computer was delivered! So not only did the 43% have nothing to do with Computers, it also had an extremely significant qualifier attached to it - inadequate insurance.

After I explained the continuous use of a statistic such as in this case, my friend and I agreed to change our conversation to another subject that had some basis in fact.

The lesson: When you hear a sensational statistic like this one, you should question its validity. It's important to validate the statistic if it is being used to build a case for your disaster recovery program with your executive management. It's better for you to validate it before you present it to executive management than to have to validate it for executive management after you have presented it. The quickest way to lose credibility with management is to misstate your case when you make your presentation. A word to the wise is sufficient.

Edward S. Devlin, CDRP, is one of disaster recovery's most experienced and respected consultants. He is Executive Vice President of SunGard Planning Solutions, and he is currently working on a book sharing his wisdom. His column is a regular feature of Disaster Recovery Journal.

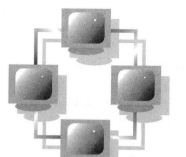

Sample Password Policy

*W*e would like to take this opportunity to share with managers and staff a few pointers on security awareness. We hope you understand the need for our security policies and procedures and apply them while using network workstations in your job. Why do we need computer security? What could happen if information you work with got into the wrong hands?

Consider the type of information you work with daily:

Customer Information. This is information that is provided to us on a confidential basis. Unauthorized access to this information could hurt both our organization and our clients.

Personnel Information. This is information that is confidential by law. Unauthorized access to this information could hurt members of our staff and expose the organization to legal liability.

Other Sensitive Data. Consider the impact if client files, accounting information, and so on got into the wrong hands.

What can you do to enhance the security of computers and the information on them? There are several things you, as an employee, can do to protect yourself as well as others:

1. Don't give your password to a co-worker or supervisor. Remember you are responsible for information entered into the system under your password. If he/she asks for your password say "NO". You have that right.

2. Don't let a co-worker or supervisor use your password. If a co-worker forgets his or her password, and you log that person on to the system under your password, you are responsible for his or her actions because data is being entered under your password.

3. Don't leave your workstation unattended. If you are called away, please remember to log off the system, or, if you have keyboard locking, lock the keyboard. It only takes a minute for someone to access critical data from your workstation. Once again, it's your password that's logged on to the system.

4. Follow established guidelines for secure passwords.

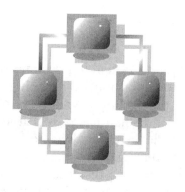

Sample E-Mail Policy

The following is a draft e-mail policy from a U.S. Government agency.

TO: All Employees
         Network Systems Administrators

FROM: Director
         Division of XXX

SUBJECT: Agency Policy on Electronic
           Mail (E-Mail)

1.   Purpose. To provide guidance to employees concerning their rights and responsibilities with respect to the proper use of agency e-mail systems.

2.   Background. E-mail has become one of the widest used forms of communication

throughout the agency. E-mail has become an indispensable business tool, easing communications, enhancing work flow, increasing productivity and performing a variety of other business functions, such as file transfer. E-mail has provided a foundation for fostering and improving employee communications. E-Mail has allowed us to reduce our telecommunications expenses by providing a no-cost and efficient alternative to long-distance telephone and fax communications. The agency encourages the business use of e-mail for all employees, but current incidents have prompted the need to create a formal policy regarding the appropriate use of e-mail and to inform employees and managers of their rights and responsibilities associated with this use. Additionally, a formal policy aids the agency in communicating appropriate procedures, in protecting against potential disclosure of sensitive information or litigation arising out of potential violations of fiduciary responsibility or invasion of privacy (employee work rights).

3.   Definitions. The following definitions apply through this Directive:

   a.   Electronic Mail System. An integrated set of computer and communications hardware and software which provides for the capability of sending messages and files between users connected to the system. E-mail systems provide for storage and later retrieval of messages and attachments, as well as real-time communication.

   b.   E-Mail. Any message which is sent electronically through one or more computers and/or communications networks and which in most cases has a human originator and receiver. This policy applies to any e-mail service which is accessible by agency employees, whether it be mainframe or local area network (LAN) based, or available to employees through on-line subscription services.

   c.   Attachment. Any file included with, or attached to an e-mail message (in some cases, the attachment may comprise the entire message sent between originator and receiver), or sent through the e-mail system.

d.   Business Day Related Communication. Any communication which occurs during the normal accomplishment of ones duties or job function. For example, it is acceptable to send a mail message to a colleague to set up a lunch appointment, but not to sell football tickets.

4.   Objectives. The agency e-mail policy is intended to allow the agency to derive the benefits of increased efficiency through the use of e-mail while insuring the protection of information assets, agency integrity, and employee rights.

5.   Scope. This policy applies to:

a.   All agency employees including permanent, temporary, part-time and contract employees, and to all other users of any agency e-mail system regardless of their affiliation.

b.   All agency owned or operated e-mail systems, or e-mail systems which are subscribed to and paid for by the agency.

c.   All e-mail messages, attachments and associated files.

6.   Policy. It is the policy of the agency that all electronic mail systems (e-mail systems) should only be used for business related or "business day" communication. E-mail systems and all e-mail generated using these systems, including their associated backups, are considered to be an asset owned by the agency and are not the property of any users of agency e-mail services regardless of whether they are employees of the agency or not.

Although it will NOT be the policy of the agency to monitor e-mail messages in general, the agency reserves the right to do so for the performance of operation, maintenance, auditing, security or investigative functions. Requests to monitor e-mail must be submitted in writing to the appropriate Division/Office Head, and employees involved in the monitoring activity are obligated to keep information observed in the monitoring process in confidence.

Network administrators and others charged with the administration, maintenance, security or operation of any agency owned system will be responsible for safeguarding employees' e-mail messages. Network administrators are not authorized, without the express permission of a user, to delete a users password so that e-mail can be read, unless they receive written instructions from their Division/Office Head to do so. If a user determines that their password has been deleted without their permission, they should immediately report this to their supervisor.

Employees should be aware that e-mail messages which have been sent to other(s) can potentially be forwarded by recipients to other users of the e-mail system, can be printed and ultimately read by anyone who sees the printed message, can be inadvertently routed to an individual other than the intended recipient and can be potentially accessed by others if PCs are unattended while log-in is active. Therefore, nothing written in an e-mail message can be guaranteed complete privacy and should be considered a part of the public record.

E-mail system users should use good judgement in forwarding mail messages and attachments that contain information that the recipient is not authorized to have access to, or contain information that could damage an individual, personally or professionally, if released to the wrong parties.

7.   Responsibilities:

   a.   Under this policy, the agency is responsible for:

      1) Informing all new employees about the agency's e-mail policy and insuring that they understand their rights and responsibilities with regard to the use of e-mail under this

policy. The Agency Services Branch will be responsible for disseminating this information.

2) Training network and system administrators and other privileged users charged with the operation, security and maintenance of agency e-mail systems and their associated hardware and software in how to discharge their function properly without violating any of the provisions herein. All Divisions/Offices performing automation/security training are responsible for this function.

3) Keeping abreast of changes in litigation which may create a need for the revision of this policy, and making the appropriate changes if and when necessitated by these changes. The Legal Division is responsible for performing this function.

4) Meeting and adhering to any union agreements or other fiduciary responsibility regarding Privacy Act Information, employee work rights and any other articles of non-disclosure which are deemed applicable.

b.   Under this policy, users of any agency provided e-mail systems are responsible for:

1) Reading and understanding this policy and its provisions, and making sure that they abide by them.

2) Using the agency e-mail system only for correspondence related to the business function and for personal gain, or for non-business related (personal) correspondence.

(3) understanding that the agency will not be liable for any disclosure of personal information in the event that the employee chooses to send such information in violation of this policy.

(4) knowing how to classify information which should not be sent through e-mail due to its sensitivity, or which should be sent through the e-mail only after it is encrypted.

(5) accessing e-mail files only as authorized in the performance of their job function.

(6) respecting the rights of other employees provided under this policy.

(7) informing management of any abuses of this policy.

7.   Disciplinary Action. Employees or systems administrators or managers who willfully or knowingly violate or otherwise abuse the provisions of this policy may be subject to disciplinary action. Managers, supervisors and systems administrators responsible for agency e-mail systems may make recommendations to Division Directors concerning policy violations. Appropriate disciplinary action will be determined by the employee's Division Director or Office Head in accordance with agency Regulations, Part 336, titled "Employee Responsibilities and Conduct".

8.   Additional Information. Questions regarding this policy should be referred to the Chief, XX Sections.

9.   Effective Date. All agency employees must comply with the terms of this directive immediately. Mainframe, LAN and other systems managers and administrators must modify system configurations and procedures, if necessary, to comply with the terms of this policy within 10 days of the date of this directive.

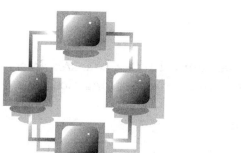

Resource Guide

*T*his Resource guide is divided into three parts:

Part 1 is a partial list of publications and services that pertain to LAN disaster prevention and recovery.

Part 2 is a list of products and services mentioned in this book.

Part 3 is a list of companies mentioned in this book.

Part I—Publications and Services for LAN Disaster Prevention and Recovery.

Note: This is a partial listing. A more comprehensive listing, as well as listings of disaster planning related products, can be found in *The Disaster Recovery Yellow Pages*, listed below under the heading *Books*.

Periodicals

Disaster Recovery Journal
The Journal Dedicated to Corporate Recovery Planning
P.O. Box 510110,
St. Louis, MO 63151
Telephone: 314-894-0276
Facsimile: 314-894-7474
Free to qualified personnel. Covers business disaster recovery issues.

Power Quality Assurance
P.O. Box 6209
Lafayette, IN 47903-6209
Telephone: 800-841-7881
                  317-497-2180
Facsimile: 317-497-3376
Free to qualified personnel. Focuses on power-related problems and solutions.

Books

Backing Up NetWare LANs
Patrick H. Corrigan
ISBN 1-55851-289-6
M&T Books
A Division of MIS Press, Inc.
115 West 18th Street
New York, NY 10111
Telephone: 212-886-9200
Facsimile: 212-807-6654
An overview of backup issues in general, with a focus on Novell's NetWare. US$26.95

Disaster Recovery Planning
Regis J. "Bud" Bates
ISBN 0-07-004128-8
McGraw-Hill, Inc.
1221 Avenue of the Americas
New York, NY 10020
Telephone: 212-512-4100
Guidelines for dealing with disaster recovery planning for telecommunications networks. US$34.95

Disaster Recovery Yellow Pages
Stephen Lewis, Ph.D., C.I.S.A.
Richard Arnold, CDRP
The Systems Audit Group, Inc.
Order Department
25 Ellison Road
Newton, MA 02159
Telephone: 617-332-3496
Facsimile: 617-449-7729
Loose leaf, quarterly updates available. A guide to available disaster recovery products and services. US$98

LAN Desktop Guide to Security
NetWare Edition
Ed Sawicki
ISBN 0-672-30085-0
Sams
A Division of Prentice Hall Computer Publishing
11711 North College
Carmel, IN 46032
Telephone: 317-581-3500
LAN Security in a NetWare environment. US$27.95

Network Security Secrets
David J. Stang, Ph.D.
Sylvia Moon
ISBN 1-56884-021-7
IDG Books Worldwide, Inc.
155 Bovet Road, Suite 310
San Mateo, CA 94402
Telephone: 415-312-0650
Facsimile: 415-358-1260
A guide to maintaining LAN security. US$49.95

PC Power Protection
Mark Waller
ISBN 0-672-22637-5
Howard W. Sams & Company
4300 West 62nd. Street
Indianapolis, IN 46228
Telephone: 800-428-SAMS
             317-298-5699
A guide to solving personal computer power problems.
US$19.95

Power Quality Analysis
Dranitz Technologies Incorporated
1000 New Durham Road
Edison, NJ 08818
Telephone: 908-287-3680
A guide to understanding and troubleshooting power quality
problems. US$75.00

Services

Comdisco Disaster Recovery Services, Inc.
6111 North River Road
Rosemont, IL 60018
Telephone: 708-698-3000
LAN and PC hot sites.

The Corrigan Group
10365 S.W. Hoodview Drive
Tigard, OR 97224
Telephone: 503-598-4787
Facsimile: 503-598-4788
CompuServe: 75170,146
Internet: 75170.146@Compuserve.com
MHS: PCorriga@TCGIS
Consulting, planning and training for LAN disaster prevention and recovery.

Ontrack Data Recovery Services
6321 Bury Drive, Suite 15-19
Eden Prairie, MN 55346
Telephone: 612-937-5161
   800-872-2599
Data recovery from damaged disk and tape media.

PowerCET Corporation
2700 Augustine Drive, Suite 178
Santa Clara, CA 95054
Telephone: 408-988-1346
Facsimile: 408-988-4869
Consulting, education and training focused on the electrical environment and its impact upon the operation of electronic equipment.

The Waller Group, Inc.
2222 Foothill Boulevard, Suite 288
La Canáda, CA 91010
Telephone: 818-957-2266
Facsimile: 818-957-2293
Computer facilities consulting with an emphasis on the electrical environment.

Part II—Products and Services Mentioned in this Book

The following is a list of products and services mentioned in this book. Company phone numbers and addresses are in the next section.

Product	Vendor
ARCserve	Cheyenne Software
ADSTAR Distributed Storage Manager	IBM
Bindview NCS	LAN Support Group
Btrieve	Novell, Inc.
Cheyenne Utilities	Cheyenne Software
Close-Up	Norton-Lambert Corporation
CMOS_SAVE	Stephen V. Genusa
DBagent	Cheyenne Software
Digital Linear Tape	Digital Equipment Corporation
ESM	Legent Corporation
Flex/QL	DataAccess Corporation
Folio Views	Folio Corporation
FOR/UPSTREAM	Innovation Data Processing
LAN Auditor	Horizons Technology, Inc.

Product	Vendor
LAN Automatic Inventory	Brightwork Development Corporation
LAN²LAN	Newport Systems Solutions
Legato Networker	Legato Systems, Inc.
Lotus 123	Lotus Development Corporation
Magic	Magic Software Enterprises, Inc.
MasterDAT	GigaTrend, Inc.
Microsoft Windows	Microsoft Corporation
MPR	Novell, Inc.
MT-350 Scanner	Microtest, Inc.
NetWare	Novell, Inc.
Network Archivist	Palindrome, Inc.
Network HQ	MAGEE Enterprises
Office Locator Kit	Microtest, Inc.
OS/2	IBM
PC Anywhere	Symantec, Inc.
PC Census	Talley Systems Corporation
PKZIP	PKWARE, Inc.
PNA	Palindrome Corporation
P-Touch	Brother International Corporation
Remote LAN Node	DCA
R&R Report Writer	Concentric Data Systems, Inc.
SAVEUSER	Wolfgang Schreiber
StorageExpress	Intel Corporation
Storage Management Services	Novell, Inc.

Product	Vendor
TCNS	Thomas-Conrad Corporation
TIMERUN	Central Point Software
Unitag	A 'n D Cable Products, Inc.
UNIX	Novell, Inc.
USER-Access	Network Systems Corporation
VINES	Banyan Systems
VISIO	Shapeware Corporation
WordPerfect	WordPerfect Corporation

Part III—Companies Mentioned in this Book

3M Corporation
Data Storage Products Division
3M Center
St. Paul, MN 55144-1000
612-733-1110

ADIC
14737 NE 87th Street
P.O. Box 2996
Redmond, WA 98052
206-881-8004

American Power Conversion Corp. (APC)
132 Fairgrounds Road
West Kingston, RI 02892
800-541-8896

A 'n D Cable Products, Inc.
5100-1B Clayton Road, Suite 302
Concord, CA 94521-3139
510-672-3005

Apple Computer, Inc.
20525 Mariani Avenue
Cupertino, CA 95014
408-996-1010

Banyan Systems Incorporated
120 Flanders Road
Westboro, MA 01581
508-898-1000

Brightwork Development
766 Shrewsbury Avenue
Jerral Center West
Tinton Falls, NJ 07724
908-530-0440

Brother International Corporation
Consumer Products Division
P.O. Box 341332
Bartlett, TN 38184-1332
800-284-4357

Central Point Software
15220 N.W. Greenbrier Parkway
Beaverton, OR 97006
503-690-2680

Cheyenne Software, Inc.
55 Bryant Avenue
Roslyn, NY 11576
516-484-5110

Compuserve Information Services
5000 Arlington Centre Boulevard
P.O. Box 20212
Columbus, OH 43220
800-848-8199
614-457-0802

Concentric Data Systems, Inc.
110 Turnpike Road
Westboro, MA 01581
508-366-1122

Cylix Corporation
2637 Townsgate Road, Suite 200
Westlake Village, CA 91361
805-379-3155

Data Access Corporation
14000 S.W. 119th Avenue
Miami, FL 33186
305-238-0012

DCA
8230 Montgomery Road
Cincinnati, OH 45236
513-745-0500

Digital Equipment Corporation
P.O. Box 1450
Littleton, MA 01460
508-486-6408

EIA/TIA
See *Electronic Industry Association / Telecommunications Industry Association*

Electronic Industry Association/Telecommunications
Industry Association
2001 Pennsylvania Avenue, NW, Suite 800
Washington, DC 20006-1813
202-457-4912

Exabyte Corporation
1685 38th Street
Boulder, CO 80301
303-447-7454

Folio Corporation
2155 North Freedom Boulevard
Suite 150
Provo, UT 84604
801-375-3700

Frye Computer Systems, Inc.
19 Temple Place
Boston, MA 02111
800-234-3793
617-247-2300

Genusa, Stephen V.
OTH Programming
149 Wheeler Road
Monroe, LA 71203

GigaTrend
2234 Rutherford Road
Carlsbad, CA 92008
619-931-9122

Hewlett Packard, Ltd.
Fulton Road, Stoke Gifford
Bristol BS12 6Q2
England

Horizons Technology, Inc.
3990 Ruffin Road
San Diego, CA 92123
619-292-8320

IBM Corporation
P.O. Box 1328
Boca Raton, FL 33432
407-433-8956

Innovation Data Processing, Inc.
275 Paterson Avenue
Little Falls, NJ 07424
201-890-7300

Intel Corporation
PCED
5200 N.E. Elam Young Parkway
Hillsboro, OR 97124-6407
503-629-6407

LAN Support Group
P.O. Box 460269
Houston, TX 77056-8269
800-749-8439
713-789-0882

Legato Systems, Inc.
260 Sheridan Avenue
Palo Alto, CA 94306
415-329-7880

Legent Corporation
2000 Park Lane
Pittsburg, PA 15275
412-494-2500

Lotus Development Corporation
55 Cambridge Parkway
Cambridge, MA 02142
617-577-8500

MAGEE Enterprises, Inc.
P.O. Box 1581
Norcross, GA 30091
404-446-6611

Magic Software Enterprises, Inc.
1200 Main Street
Irvine, CA 92714
714-250-1718

Maxell Corporation of America
22-08 Route 208
Fair Lawn, NJ 07410
201-794-5900

Microsoft Corporation
One Microsoft Way
Redmond, WA 98052
206-882-8080

Microtest, Inc.
3519 East Shea Boulevard
Phoenix, AZ 85028
602-971-6464

Network Systems Corporation
7600 Boone Avenue North
Minneapolis, MN 55428
800-338-0122
612-424-4888

Newport Systems Solutions
4019 Westerly Place
Newport Beach, CA 92660
800-368-6533
714-752-1511

Novell, Inc.
122 East 1700 South
Provo, UT 84606
801-429-7000
800-453-1267

ONEAC Corporation
27944 North Bradley Road
Libertyville, IL 60048
708-816-6000

Ontrack Computer Systems, Inc.
6321 Bury Drive, Suite 15-19
Eden Prairie, MN 55346
612-937-1107

Palindrome Corporation
600 East Diehl Road
Naperville, IL 60563
708-505-3300

Panamax
150 Mitchell Blvd.
San Rafael, CA 94903-2057
415-499-3900

PKWARE, Inc.
7545 N. Port Washington Road, Suite 205
Glendale, WI 53217
BBS: 414-352-7176

Schreiber, Dr. Wolfgang
Schanzenstr. 74
4000 Dusseldorf Germany
Fax: (1149) - 211 - 55 64 69

Shapeware Corporation
1601 5th Avenue, Suite 800
Seattle, WA 98101-1625
206-467-6723

Siemon Company
76 Westbury Park Road
Watertown, CT 06795-0400
203-274-2523

Sony Corporation Of America
655 River Oaks Parkway
San Jose, CA 95134
408-944-4301

Tally Systems Corporation
Buck Road, P.O. Box 70
Hanover, NH 03755
603-643-1300

Thomas-Conrad Corporation
1908-R Kramer Lane
Austin, TX 78758
512-836-1935

WordPerfect Corporation
1555 North Technology Way
Orem, UT 84057
800-451-5151
International: 801-222-4200

X-Tree Corporation
See *Central Point Software*

Index